BENEDICT ANDREWS: COLLECTED PLAYS

Benedict Andrews

COLLECTED PLAYS

OBERON BOOKS
LONDON

WWW.OBERONBOOKS.COM

First published in 2016 by Oberon Books Ltd
521 Caledonian Road, London N7 9RH
Tel: +44 (0) 20 7607 3637 / Fax: +44 (0) 20 7607 3629
e-mail: info@oberonbooks.com
www.oberonbooks.com

A catalogue record for this book is available from the British
Library.

PB ISBN: 9781783199457
E ISBN: 9781783199464

Cover image © Caroline Walker, 'Pool Party', oil on linen,
167 x 240cm, 2012

Visit www.oberonbooks.com to read more about all our books
and to buy them. You will also find features, author interviews and
news of any author events, and you can sign up for e-newsletters
so that you're always first to hear about our new releases.

Contents

Introduction

I.

The roles are basically clear: a playwright writes a play. The actors learn the lines, and the director creates a world in which the text and the actors can flourish. If someone changes sides it is usually the actors. This is probably due to the nature of their talent, their gift for being able to change. That is why actors sometimes become directors, and sometimes they also write plays. Most of the time, after having written one or two plays, they return to the stage again and take on different roles, abandoning that of the playwright.

Sometimes playwrights change sides as well and become directors. Because they are frustrated with what the directors are doing with their plays, or because they do not want to hand over their work after they have finished the writing process and want to see it through rehearsals themselves. Here, too, the changing of sides is rarely permanent, there are many things to be said in favour of the division of labour and of an artistic collective.

It is much more rare that directors change sides. Actually I only know of Benedict Andrews. The other directors I talk to about the possibility of writing plays themselves are usually disgusted and dismissive: they say they are catastrophically untalented, someone else needs to take care of the writing. They want to enter into a dialogue with the text, sometimes even into a conflict. And such a creative rivalry with oneself demands more of a split personality than anyone could ask for.

Benedict Andrews is a different case. And yet his story could be told very simply: you could say that this is a theatre director who has such a wealth of theatre experience that even in his first play, *Every Breath*, he emerges as a fully-formed playwright. As if writing was a way of carrying on directing, a reverse movement. As if with each play he wants to lay the basis for yet another magically iridescent Andrews show. And it is true that each of his plays can be read as an ideal starting point for a production by the director Benedict Andrews: the shimmering, oppressive eroticism of *Every Breath*, the fierce loneliness of *Like a Sun*, the surreal poetry of *The Stars*, and the methodical analysis of *Geronimo*. The worlds of these plays appear to be fed by the visual language of the director, who has spent years depicting the strangeness of our world in ever-changing, sometimes drastic images. Who, long before others started copying him, directed plays set completely behind glass, as if the people we are watching are precious reptiles devouring each other, who has swathed the dream worlds of Calderón in reflecting gold, who let the glowing days of Sarsaparilla play out in double or triple exposure in a single house. Whose Blanche in *A Streetcar Named Desire* was a sister to his Grace in Sarah Kane's *Cleansed*, both of them sisters to his Richard II in *The War of the Roses* (his marathon staging of Shakespeare's history plays.) All of these are characters who seem to have dropped out of their societies and who are considered mad by their fellow human beings. In Benedict Andrews' world they are amazed strangers who no longer understand their surroundings, until we too no longer understand our world and are able to take home this not-being-able-to-understand as a precious insight. So it is possible to explain Benedict Andrews' plays through his work as a director, as a continuation of his exploration of the strange in the familiar. And this kind of explanation would not be wrong either except, perhaps, for the assumption that these are plays that can only flourish in the hands of the director Benedict Andrews. And yet his plays are more than the coagulation of his theatre experience. They are more than serviceable springboards for a writing director. More than the tennis ball the player throws himself in order to serve an ace. In the case of Benedict Andrews we have to say goodbye to the notion that someone has changed sides. Because in the case of Benedict Andrews those sides do not really exist.

II.

The widows no longer have the energy to always carry the watering cans they use to water the plants on the graves of their husbands all the way from their homes to the graveyard. They have hung them on a metal construction, a kind of carpet rod with hooks. Some of them have written their names on the bottoms of the watering cans so they do not get stolen, but no one really steals here in the graveyard anyway. Now the watering cans are hanging by the entrance to the graveyard, next to the water tap used for filling them. The colourful plastic is set off by the dark green of the conifers behind them, between the trees you can glimpse the moss-covered gravestones.

Benedict Andrews took this photo in 2004. He has come to Berlin to direct Sarah Kane's *Cleansed* at the Schaubühne. His camera is a Japanese model intended for tourists, cheap, nothing special, a bit impractical – you have to switch off the flash manually so it does not erupt into every picture. But the camera is small and handy, he always carries it with him. On his walks through the city – he always walks – he takes photos of a Berlin I have never seen before. He sees things of whose existence I am vaguely aware, but I would simply have walked past them in the street without recognising them. He sees the shop window of the wig-maker's where all the mannequin heads with the same face and different hairstyles are staring in the same direction, he sees the last remnants of the GDR aesthetic in shops and bars, he climbs through a hole in the fence of the abandoned fairground and takes photos of the huge, overgrown dinosaur figures long before this enchanted place becomes a photo location for album covers and fashion shoots. Again and again he also simply takes photos of the light itself. The light that falls on a wet tree or makes the air shimmer between two *plattenbau* apartment blocks. He photographs a city familiar to me, that I have lived in for years, in a way that makes me feel as if I am seeing it for the first time, as if it is only his view of my city that makes me realise why this city is the way it is. Through his photos he makes me see it as he does. The way he sees it is via a stranger's perspective on something familiar. A way of seeing that makes something visible that otherwise would have remained invisible forever. Back then I thought this ability was due to the fact that he, as an Australian, had more of a distance, and that this distance enabled him not to miss the forest for the trees. Now I think differently. He has long since become something other than an Australian travelling the world. He has lived in Berlin, worked in London and New

York, found a new home between the volcanoes of Iceland and adapted his external way of life to his inner sensibility, which I can perhaps best describe as that of an alien. He is a stranger everywhere, as if he was from another planet, because being a stranger corresponds to an emotion he carries inside him. I have witnessed how, in a city he had never set foot in before, he was literally able to smell a shop with second hand records: on one of our walks through Munich he suddenly lifted his head and said: "there has to be a record shop here somewhere." And in fact not two hundred metres away there *was* a shop, and Benedict disappeared inside in order to browse through rare disco records. As an alien he has developed the ability to read the poetic matrix of a city. In 2008 we were in wintery Melbourne in order to work on our joint production, *Moving Target*. Here, as with all his shows, Andrews filled the rehearsal space, an abandoned church, with his own language, his own sense of humour, his own code, which infuses the banalities of the everyday with meaning and casts them into a light that makes them unfamiliar, as if you are seeing them for the first time. The actor who hides under a table becomes an ironic sculpture, the whole space becomes a sinister crime scene, it is an infectious transformation of reality that becomes addictive once you have taken part in it, a constant shift in perception that does not stop even when you leave the rehearsal space. The words someone has written on the fogged-up mirror in the bathroom of his hotel room, "BENJAMIN", are a message from a hotel ghost that haunts the building and sets off the fire alarm at night, that refuses to be turned off even when you knock the beeping apparatus from the ceiling. The whole town is wrapped in dense fog, on our way to the rehearsal we pass a house on Gertrude Street from whose basement, probably from a laundry room, rises dense steam, and it is obvious: all of the fog hanging above Melbourne originates from this one laundry room in Gertrude Street. Part of the laughter about this idea is always amazement at a world that only reveals its beauty if you are prepared to see it with the eyes of an alien. In the past one might have called these eyes of an alien the gift of a poet, and consequently it comes as no surprise that Benedict Andrews does not just direct theatre and opera but also writes plays and award-winning poems, takes photos and makes films. Here, there are no sides to change. All the different ways of artistic expression are nourished by the same perception and the search for expression stems from the same impetus.

III.

Theatre can do lots of things. It can entertain, stir, teach, agitate for a cause. It is about failed designs for life, about fulfilled and – more frequently – unfulfilled love, about the relationship of the individual to society, about the expectations we have of others and ourselves. In its most successful moments theatre is a place of recognition. This recognition can come from the simple mechanism of identification: we identify with a character on stage and through watching the action on stage experience what following the actions of this character would mean in reality. And because in theatre we are confronted with the consequences of these actions we go through an experience that enriches us without having to suffer the consequences in our own lives. The playwright's trick consists of the fact that he offers us a character for identification whose moral principles or situation in life are very different from our own. And thus we can delight in the amoral actions of Richard III without having to shout for a horse at the end. We can live through the excesses of Othello's jealousy without having strangled our own wife at the end. We suffer the torture of a ruined life with Hedda Gabler without having to shoot ourselves at the end. We enter the safe space of the theatre and experience something we can neither afford to nor want to do in our real lives. But we carry this experience we have gone through emotionally from the protected space of the theatre and into our own lives, where it continues to exist as a recognition that we too could be a Richard, an Othello, a Hedda. Thus the theatre is a place where our consciousness experiences things in laboratory-like conditions that we try to avoid in our real lives. That we are afraid of, but that we unconsciously seek out because they are a mirror of our unconscious wishes, aggressions and desires.

Benedict Andrews' plays stealthily seep into our unconscious. They consist of elements that seem familiar to us: a family constellation, people driving in a car at night, people in the gym, in a waiting area at an airport. Their language is our language, they are talking about things we have talked about. But in these apparently familiar dialogues lurks a strangeness, something unfamiliar, surprising. The alien does not miss the forest for the trees and shows us his view of the strange creature we wake up next to in the morning, the unreality of an actual manhunt, of the insidious loneliness by the pool, the physical brutality of a capitalist concentration of power. It is an incorruptible view, it registers but is never cold or judgemental but full of interest and affection for the creatures it perceives. And by letting us see through his eyes he enables us to look at ourselves. We become strangers to ourselves in the same way we become strangers to ourselves when we murder with Richard or make a mess of our lives with Hedda Gabler. It is the strangeness of an alien that opens the doors to a theatrical recognition and that confronts us with the question of what we are and what we want to be.

by Marius von Mayenburg
Translated by Maja Zade

LIKE A SUN

Clarity *(claritas)* can be thought of in two ways: like the shimmering of gold (due to its density) or like the splendour of crystal (due to its transparency.) According to Gregory the Great, the bodies of the blessed possess clarity in both senses: they are diaphanous like a crystal and impervious to light like gold. It is this halo of light, which emanates from the glorious body, that can be perceived by a non-glorious body, and its splendour can differ according to the quality of the blessed. The greater or lesser clarity of the halo is the outermost index of the differences between the glorious bodies.

Giorgio Agamben

Characters

DAVID, 40 plus

KANE, barely 20

KEV, in his 50s

GUY, in his 20s

A PACK OF MEN, various ages

AMELIA, late 20s

ANDREW, around 30

TROY, 9

AVRIL, 11

LAURA, mid 20s

THOSE MACHINES

Concrete room.

DAVID, alone.

DAVID	Okay. So. Last night when I left here, I
	went to a bar and sat on a glass terrace
	overlooking the harbour. I drank a beer
	and checked out this woman sipping
	chardonnay, alone. She looked –

	He stares.

	I dunno –

	Still staring.

	She looked like you.

	Snaps out of it.

	I asked mind if I join you. She did not. So
	we ordered more drinks and ate salty nuts
	from a bowl the waiter deposited on the
	table. The city glittered in the harbour's
	inky waters and the sultry night made our
	clothes all sticky. We licked our fingers
	which were salty from the nuts. Licked 'em
	clean.

	Grins.

	When the bar shut, we were both pretty
	drunk. She told the driver where to drive
	and we sat, knees pressed together, as the
	car sped through the empty streets of the
	glassy city. I dragged my lips down her
	neck. She stuck her tongue in my mouth.
	And neither of us cared if the driver snuck
	glances in the rear-view mirror when I slid
	my hand up her skirt, slipped her panties
	aside and eased a finger into her pussy.

The amber street lamps shining through the branches of the overhanging trees cast filigree shadows on the road.

Closes eyes.

Like the lace-work of her pretty panties where my fingers played.

Smiles. Savours.

Filigree.

Opens eyes.

Nice.

Flexes.

I tipped the driver – that filthy cunt – and followed her to the lobby. She swayed, a bit drunk, tight skirt hugging her ass, then punched a code into a security pad and up, up, up we rode in the elevator's mirrored cabin, endlessly reflected. I had the feeling I'd met her, seen her before, but for my sweet life I couldn't place her and she never mentioned it. At the door, she dug around in her purse for keys. Time kinda stopped. She swayed. Her skirt rode up. Her hands trembled –

He looks at his hands.

Like fluttering doves.

Freezes.

I don't know why. They just did. Okay?

Stares.

In we went and –

Snaps out of it.

Pretty quickly, it became clear we weren't alone. Another woman emerged from a dim hallway and was introduced as the drunk girl's mother. This is a turn-up for the books, I thought or said as we exchanged pleasantries over a crisp Sav Blanc. We sat real close on their soft, white sofa. The huge flatscreen on mute – a bombing, a beauty pageant. Mutti put on music to set the mood. Easy listening, jazzy, nice. Excuse me. Sorry. Just a sec.

He fetches a stick – the width and length of a halved broomstick or a snapped pool cue – with which he performs various exercises during the following.

Both women removed their shoes and encouraged me to do the same. The daughter flipped channels on the silent telly while her mum and I discussed the ups and downs of business, market fluctuations. On TV, bikini-clad dancers with cherry red lips gyrated in an aircraft hanger as gold dust rained down. A chanteuse crooned away on the hi-fi. The weird synchronicity of her song and the choreography on the screen held us hypnotised. As if time had slowed right down, nearing its last instant. It was completely fucking beautiful.

Freezes.

I think it was the mother who first began to strip. Sorry I can't remember such an important detail, we were kinda drunk. Maybe the mother removed the daughter's clothes? Can't remember. Sorry.

Resumes exercises.

Anyway, I was in between mother and daughter. Kissing both, touching both. Multitasking.

Attack moves.

Ever made love to two people simultaneously? Well, it requires real concentration. You get into it intensely with one, you have to be mindful that the other one doesn't feel excluded. The whole thing's intensified when you're with a pair of lovers who are related – siblings for example – but it's especially intricate when a mother and daughter are involved. Imagine all the subterranean stuff going on there.

Rapid tempo moves.

I was busy with that – sucking mutti's titties, reaching back to slap her daughter's ass, both real nasty, grinding, rubbing their pussies like crazy – when suddenly, I found myself worrying if the daughter – who had after all been the one to bring me home in the first place – was getting the idea that I preferred her mum's tits to hers, so I'd abandon mama's and start on the daughter's. Or vice versa. Making sure everyone was good. A picture of concentration. Like one of those Chinese acrobats juggling plates.

Slows.

I don't mean for it to sound like a big deal or some kind of hassle. No way. We were making each other feel real nice. My head was in the mother's lap sucking on her cunt – hope you don't mind me telling you this – and her daughter was feasting on my cock when all of a sudden it struck me that where I was tonguing and pleasuring this moaning woman was the exact place that my other lover – the woman with my cock in her mouth – had come from. Literally. Her point of absolute origin.

Becoming still now.

This radical intimacy made me feel ridiculously happy in a way that overleaped the pleasures and sensations of the sex act. I felt in touch with the whole cycle of creation. I briefly tasted – pardon the pun – the absolute mystery of birth.

Shrieks with pure, animal joy.

Yes! I'm a god, bitches!

Now his exercises take on a kind of ecstatic, even holy quality.

We moved from the sofa into mummy's bedroom and I made love to them both. Any anxieties about who was with who fell away. There can be so much confusion, so much animosity in families, but when mother and daughter looked into each other's blissed-out eyes, there was nothing but joy. Their faces, so alike despite the difference of years, radiated pure, unadulterated joy. All day long, I've felt traces of that ecstasy lingering in my bones. A remainder of the part I played in their happiness. I'm still glowing.

Exercises for a while in silence.

Focus. Stay Sharp.

Slow, concentrated movements.

9

You look great by the way. Like what you've
done with your hair. Makes you look less
stern. No, not stern. Critical. Yeah, you look
right through me. With your X-ray vision.

Silence. Exercise.

I'm older than I ever thought I'd be. Never
thought I'd make it past thirty. Let alone
forty. But here I am. Fighting fit. Top of my
game.

Sharp move.

A mate called today. Wanted my services.
To internationalise his brand basically. And
don't get me wrong, he's got a good stable
– nice young cunt. But I can't take on new
stuff right now. Not with everything else.
But my oh my, he's a tenacious fuck. Kept
at me. Trying to sweeten up his offer. Know
what? I laughed in his fat fuck face. Told
him, man you're so *motherfucking* short-term
vision, in terms of your operational ethics,
you slippery cunt. And he laughed too,
fucking shat himself. Because he knew that
even with everything I'm dealing with I am
absolutely not to be fucked with.

Silence. He rests. Stillness.

Operational ethics. Fuck yeah. Wait. Back
in a sec.

*He fetches another stick, nearly identical to the first.
Under the following he performs an increasingly
complex series of manoeuvres.*

As a boy of eleven, for one weekend, I
was left in the care of some people I only
vaguely knew. Business associates of my
father. Or people he knew socially. Maybe

he sat next to them at some dinner. Anyway, they had a house an hour or so from the city where they raised horses. And two sons. About my age. Dad drove me down a long driveway through a thick, green forest toward a two-storey silver house. He exchanged pleasantries with the smiling owners of the silver house, unloaded my bags and drove off. Left me there. In the depths of the forest.

Hypnotic circular patterns with both sticks.

The brothers galloped toward me, hitched their horses, shook my hand. Apparently we went to the same school, even attended the same classes. Because they were banging on about various teachers and classmates we supposedly had in common. But I can't picture them at my school. I only see them there, that weekend, dressed in matching riding hats, crisp white shirts, jodhpurs and shiny black boots. As if they'd stepped out of a worn photograph.

Slow patterns.

Those boys, like their parents, were fond of displaying their teeth when they smiled. Like this –

He demonstrates.

Little cunts.

Attack moves with the sticks.

They showed me their rooms, showed me the stupid antique toys they collected. Then off we went to explore the property. On foot. I was never offered a horse to ride. I would've liked that. But oh no, we fuckin' well walked. Them in their fancy riding gear, as if they'd rather be trotting along secret trails in the misty forests. They were like weird porcelain dolls. If we fell while racing each other down a gully or through the pines, I'd tear elbows, knees and bleed, the brothers would chip, splinter and fracture.

Slows moves.

They led me to a derelict house on a neighbouring property, and even though we had to climb a barbed wire fence, they assured me it was fine to be on the neighbour's land, he was cool with them taking a look around whenever. This old run-down place. Overgrown with blackberries. Roof collapsed, furniture black with dust. Dead leaves. Weeds in the windows, bath, sink, the beds. We prowled around, ate blackberries in the bedroom, stained our mouths purple.

Staccato moves.

It was the older boy who said it was okay to take a few things if I wanted, they did it all the time, no-one cared. I inspected scungy shelves and drawers thick with spider webs. Got an old biscuit tin with a windmill on its lid, a few marbles, a shard of blue glass, an ivory chess piece. The younger kid wanted to take a clock carved with hunting scenes but big bro forbade it. Too heavy or something.

The exercises develop into increasingly aggressive combat manoeuvres.

This old guy rode up on a trail-bike. The neighbour. Screaming. Obscenities. We took off, fast, but you can't out run a dirt-bike and soon he was on us, spit trailing from his mouth, stick in his hand – a branch of thorny brush – swiping at us as we ran stumbled and tried not to fall. The thorns stung us. The air stank of diesel. He thrashed and thrashed and thrashed.

He's brutal with the sticks now. Military precision.

When we reached the edge of his lands, he circled back, and we scrambled over the fence and kept running until he was gone. The brothers were crying. Fat glistening tears streaked their porcelain cheeks. And they howled. Like bitches. I didn't cry. I wanted to go back and knock him off his bike and hurt him like he hurt us. I wanted to hurt the brothers for not warning me about the man. And because they were howling like bitches. But I didn't touch them. We hiked home through the silent forest as evening fell.

Slowing his routine. Razor sharp concentration.

Back at the silver house, the parents weren't smiling any more. Oh no. The brothers got sent to their rooms. I was sat down, made to empty my pockets and give up any objects I'd held onto during the chase.

Slows.

The parents reprimanded me for leading their precious sons astray, for abusing their hospitality.

Comes to a stop.

They called me piece of shit, scumbag.

He puts the sticks down.

But I was smart. I snuck this –

He takes a chess piece from his pocket. A king.

– into my sock.

He balances the chess piece on his palm.

I keep it to remind me to never forget that
silver house in the forest where my father
left me that weekend. To never forget the
hate I felt for those porcelain brothers
with tear-stained cheeks. To never forget
what I decided right then and there – to
do whatever it takes to be king and to stay
king.

Closes his fist over the chess piece.

I keep this as a reminder. Of my operational
ethics.

He rests. Drinks a sports drink. Towels himself.

Did I tell you all that before?

Towels himself.

Nah, didn't think so.

*Another man, KANE, enters with a similar set of
sticks. They eye each other off then the fight is on. Very
quick concentrated sparing.*

KANE   Keep your weight forward. Don't tilt back.
That's it. Nice.

*They fight for a while. It's pretty intense. Now with
a quick succession of moves, David disarms Kane
and pins him to the floor, stands over him, stick at*

his throat. Actually, it's not really clear if David overpowered Kane or if Kane let him win.

DAVID   Gotcha.

He releases KANE and helps him up.

Thanks for today, Kane. That was great. I really enjoyed it.

KANE   No worries. See you in a bit.

DAVID   Okey-dokey, champ.

KANE leaves DAVID alone again.

Are you getting what you need here? Hope you're getting good material. Like I said, if we're gonna do this, let's do it right.

DAVID checks his watch.

The kids? Tomorrow. They're here tomorrow. Someone's picking them up. Nah, their mother's coming separately. Kids're flying solo. Well why the fuck not? Do 'em good. Yeah I know I said they'd be here when we began but it's just me for now alright? They'll be here soon. Family. Family's sacrosanct.

Takes out his phone.

I'm gonna give this woman a call. You'll like her. Face looks like she sucked too much cock and she rarely takes her sunglasses off, but I get hard just looking at her.

He laughs like a hyena.

I'm gonna call her.

He calls, wanders around talking like an actor on a phone.

KANE returns with a bucket and some towels. He uses steaming water to clean the area where they fought. Especially the spot where DAVID pinned him down.

Still on the phone, DAVID looks over KANE's shoulder to inspect his work. Pats him encouragingly on the back, ruffles his hair.

Boys nearly ready? All warmed up?

KANE   Yeah. Think so.

DAVID   Good. Get 'em to bring the gear on.

KANE   Yep.

KANE finishes. Leaves.

DAVID wanders round talking on the phone. Hangs up.

DAVID   She's gonna come, not now – on her way to Paris now – then she's gonna come. Paris with some boyfriend. Ha.

He laughs, genuinely amused.

Nice.

A group of men bring on exercise equipment. Running machines, exercise bikes, gymnastic equipment, punching bags, weights, machines etc.

I told you about the lucid dreaming, right? About the exercises and the control I gained of my dreaming. Well sometimes, I make sure she's there in my dreams and I fuck the living shit out of her.

Grinning to the one of the boys.

I don't know how anyone goes on without gaining control of their dreams. It's a waste of sleep.

He starts to use one of the exercise machines. When the men have finished setting up, they use the machines too.

You have to picture reality – your so-called reality – as a series of interlocking ideas. These ideas are all locked up together so they appear as uniform reality. The trick is to separate them, to break your surroundings down into components. Like for instance, this room. Look around. Now try to separate the elements that compose it. Look at each object – where it's positioned, what its function is, what it's connected to, what it's composed of – see it in relation to the other objects. I want you to imagine a network of objects. A *relational field.* Now focus on the room itself. Consider it as a kind of shell. Feel the volume of air contained in the shell, be aware of negative space. Okay now, imagine the architecture of the room in blueprint form. A scheme of vectors and planes, solids and voids. Strip away the surfaces. Yes they matter, but they're something we'll learn to change – skins. For now concentrate on seeing the bones of the room. Analyse shapes. Look for the essential geometry. Learn to unlock it. Are there people in the room? Look right through them. Like those machines at the airport which scan inside people. Look around. Everything's moving, everything's in constant motion, even the things – the monumental things – that you're used to seeing as motionless, fixed, still. Walls, buildings, mountains. Read the movement of things. Make a habit of it. And guess what? You've already guessed it, I'm sure. The things we're going to be constantly clocking the movement of are the so-called *living things.* Animals, insects, and humans. You know this. It's not news. We all do it all the time but we forget we're doing it because our way of being in the world has become habitual and lazy. I need you to become constantly aware. Okay? I want you to develop a voice in your brain – a kind of assistant – like when you're driving a car with GPS and the computer's firm but polite voice warns you that a turn is coming up. Get this voice to analyse the movement of humans, insects, and animals in your vicinity. Do it constantly. It's what I used to do when I started out. Before I got advanced. I used this voice to scan any movement around me. 'Hey David, see how that elbow hinges as it places the bowl of salty nuts on the table.' Got it? Good. Let's go. Get this voice working overtime when you begin. With discipline and constant application, you won't need to rely on it forever. As you gradually replace your sluggish methods of being in the world with more enhanced perception, accurate readings of the movement of animals, insects, humans and objects in your field of perception will become so-called second nature. There's a lot going on in this room, right? The guys are exercising their bodies. It's a lot to take in. So let's zoom in. Look at Kane. Remember Kane?

DAVID watches KANE exercise.

This is useful for a beginner. The way he repeats the movement.

Watches.

18

The micro-actions that come together to
generate the impression of an exercising
man. *(To KANE.)* Nice, Kane. Keep at it.

KANE smiles, keeps at it.

See the sugars burn? The blood pumping?
His lungs expanding and contracting like
an accordion? What about heat? Can you
see in infrared? Is he glowing? What're
his eyes doing? Ha! Look! See his pupils
contract? Nice. What's his mouth doing, his
tongue? See him swallow? Nostrils flaring?
And what about his busy little fingers?
Learn to scan. We move through waking
life like combs, picking up material for our
dreams. You've got to start to sift that info.

KANE has finished his reps. He rests. He's still.

Hey Kane. Come forward for us, would you.
You mind?

KANE shakes his head – no problem.

Now just walk around a bit.

KANE   What like this?

He walks around.

DAVID   Yeah something like that.

Watches KANE walking around.

I mean this is fairly basic. He's not doing
much. Just walking.

Watches him for a bit.

Less weaving Kane okay. Try something more
basic. Just walk back and forwards a bit.

KANE walks backwards.

No. Wait. Kane. Not actually backwards. I mean up and down. Like walk toward the front then turn around and walk back then do it again until I tell you to stop. Okay?

KANE does that.

Yeah. Like that. Better. Yeah.

Watches KANE walking back and forwards.

You're a bit stiff or something. Can you make it more natural. Just walking.

KANE   What like this?

KANE tries.

How's that?

DAVID   Yeah, nah. You're walking all weird. Like a cartoon character. That purple dog what's-his-name. Jesus Kane. Okay what if to make it more natural, you imagine you're actually walking somewhere. Picture where you're walking, then walk how you'd walk there. Okay?

KANE walking for a bit.

What are you doing? Why're you moving your head all the time?

KANE   I'm looking at the birds.

DAVID   What birds?

KANE   The little birds singing in their nests in the branches of the trees.

DAVID   What're you going on about Kane?

KANE   You said –

DAVID	Kane, why are you holding your hand out like that?
KANE	You asked me to imagine I was actually walking somewhere so I pictured myself strolling through the forest on my way to post a letter to a friend.

He keeps walking like he's on his way through the forest to post a letter.

DAVID	Okay Kane, stop.

KANE doesn't seem to hear. He's completely absorbed with his stroll.

Kane!

KANE	Huh? What?
DAVID	Kane stop walking!
KANE	Huh? What? Why?
DAVID	Kane just stop. Stop walking now. Okay? Kane? KANE!

KANE stops.

It's not working. Like that. With the letter. Maybe just try thinking of nothing while you walk. Just blank. Okay.

KANE walks again.

Kane stop.

KANE stops.

You've still got the letter in your hand. Drop the letter .

KANE drops the letter.

Good. Now relax and just think of nothing. Okay?

KANE   Okay.

                Pause.

                Ready?

                DAVID nods. KANE takes a deep breath.

                I'm off.

                *KANE walks backward and forward trying to think
                of nothing.*

DAVID   Don't forget to breathe Kane.

                *KANE walks backward and forward, trying to think
                of nothing, trying to remember to breathe.*

                Can you try closing your eyes?

KANE   Really? You sure?

DAVID   Just do it Kane.

                *DAVID watches KANE walking back and forwards
                with his eyes closed.*

                Okay. Good. That's good. Keep going, keep
                going Kane.

                He watches KANE walking around with closed eyes.

                Yeah. Like that. Yeah.

                He watches KANE walking.

                Watch Kane walk. Analyse. Please separate
                the physical actions – the ones that your
                special voice is reminding you to constantly
                observe – from the emotional signals that
                Kane's body is transmitting about how he's
                feeling right now. Is he relaxed or tense?
                Comfortable or out of place? Is Kane being
                straight with us or is he trying to hide
                something?

KANE walks around nervously.

Scan him with your X-ray eyes. Good. Okay, now you might want to use another voice to remind you to stay informed about the emotional signals. Make this voice different from the one you've already got for movement analysis. A different gender or a different regional accent. I like different gender. But do what you feel. One voice for basic movements. Another for emotional information. (*Does the new voice, robotic female.*) 'Observe hesitation in subject. Possible sign of nervous agitation.' Watch Kane. Break him down into components.

Pause.

Good.

Pause.

Now, let's take it up a notch. *(To the other men.)* Guys, can you help out for a bit?

The guys listen.

Okay stop what you're doing and walk around for a bit like Kane. That'd be great. Thanks. Eyes shut.

They do.

Great. Thanks. Good on you guys. No peeking now. Good. That's it.

He watches the men.

Doesn't have to be just back and forwards anymore. Relax that idea. Move around how you like but stay nice and easy. That's good. Hey good, you're doing great.

He watches the men moving about, their eyes closed.

23

Okay, so get those voices going. There's a lot to take in I know, but keep at it. Break the movement down, sift it for emotional content. This is just basic stuff you'll need if you want to stop being a passive dreamer. Do you really want to stay a passive dreamer? Do you want to keep wasting your dreams?

Checks watch.

You have to learn to take control of everything around you okay and a big step is learning to identify the real dream protagonists. Let me repeat that. You have to learn to recognise your lead actors. Who's the key player and who's just an extra? Who's there to fill the background out – make it more believable – and who's there to relate with, really go deeper with?

Watches guys moving around – something hypnotic in their movement.

Stay solid. Listen to your voices. All part of step one. Basic awareness. Okay. *(To the men.)* Thanks guys. That was great. Give yourselves a big pat on the back. Well done.

The guys stop walking around. They take a little break. Drink sports drinks. Towel down. Then get back to work on the machines.

Yeah and the other awareness that I want to mention today is of course *time* and *place*. We talked about it before so it's a reminder. You've probably already been working on this so don't mind me if I go through it again. Okay. Controlling your dreams is pretty wild but it's a lot of work and not everyone's up for that, especially

all the extra care you have to take, i.e.
the procedures you have to install in your
waking life. You have to learn to remind
yourself, I'm awake now, okay. Please
be super-aware. It's not enough to coast
through life anymore. You can't switch off,
okay. You gotta check and double check –
what's happening now, what might happen,
work backwards, how did you get to this
place, keep a mental log. Okay? Stay on
it, don't slip. Oh and you better make sure
your watch is working.

He taps his watch.

Stay exact. Remember that, okay. You need
to protect yourself from the risk of getting
lost in dream, of confusing waking life and
dream. Use your watch okay. Clock the
time. Backtrack. Make a checklist. I don't
want you getting lost.

A long silence.

When she's finished in Paris she'll come
here and I'll fuck her brains out.

Silence.

I get lonely. When the kids aren't here.
When my wife's away. So yes of course, I
look forward to Amelia coming from Paris.

Pause.

That's her name, Amelia.

Pause.

Amelia. Amelia.

The guys working out.

25

(Speaking to one of the guys.) Hey Kev, how's tricks?

KEV   Not too shabby, Dave.

DAVID And the family?

KEV   Good thanks Dave, all good. The boys're big, nearly finished school.

DAVID And Cheryl?

KEV   Great. Cheryl's great.

DAVID Tell her I asked after her won't you.

KEV   Yep sure. No worries.

DAVID Looking good Kev, real cut. Keep at it.

KEV   Will do, Dave, thanks.

DAVID Me and Kev – we go way back, right Kev?

KEV   Yep.

DAVID Kev was working here when I took over. Had to let the dead wood go. But not Kev. Big Kev wasn't dead wood. I wanted him on my team then and I want him on my team now. A storm's coming and I need top guys beside me. Guys like Kev.

Silence. The men are working out.

Guys like Kev make me feel the burden of management. It's on me to take care of him and the other boys so they can take care of their people. Kev's got Cheryl, his sons. Everyone's got someone, right guys?

He takes the chess piece out from his pocket.

The king is the lonely one. The king never rests. He holds it together. All this –

He gestures to his surroundings. In the silence, one guy performs quick manoeuvres on the pommel horse.

Behind the royal façade, behind the pomp
and circumstance, is mess and torment,
life lived in fear. He looks at his troops and
wonders who's been sent to kill him. He
checks over his shoulder for the assassin. Is
this any life? He'd swap with the plainest
man, swap his riches to be a normal guy
curled up on a sofa binge watching the latest
long-form TV drama. You can tell me that
the pleasures of being king outweigh all
others but I tell you that to live surrounded
by scandal, holding onto what you've got
with both hands, beset by worry, no longer
holds any shine for me.

He lifts his arms in divine supplication. Eyes to heaven.

I pray we will weather the storm.

The men sing – Monteverdi, Madrigali Guerrieri et Amorosi : Libro Ottavo.

MEN   Altri canti d'Amor, tenero arciero,
I dolci vezzi, e I sosprati baci;
narri gli sdengi e le bramate paci
quand'unisce due alme un sol pensiero.

Di Marte io canto, furibondo e fiero,
iduri incontri e le battaglie audaci;
strider le spade, e bombeggiar le faci'
fo nel mio canto belli'coso e fiero.
Tu cui tessuta han di Cesare alloro
la corona immortal Marte e Bellona,
gradite il verde ancor novo lavoro,

che mente guerre canta e guerre sona,
o gran Fernando, l'orgoglioso choro
del tuo sommo valor canta e ragiona.

The light turns cold. While the men sing, David works out on various apparatus. He balances on the balance beam. He hangs from the gymnastic rings. He climbs on the horizontal bars. He sits like a lonely ape.

DAVID   Okay guys, let's work.

The men stop and listen to DAVID.

Now you all know I like to smash the competition, right? I like it like some people like driving fast cars or cultivating exotic plants or making love in public. I like it. It's my thing. It's how we do. Like for example this guy –

A guy enters.

He's the competition.

The men rearrange themselves.

Well, he jobs for the competition, so he's the competition right?

The men nod.

His name's Guy and we're gonna smash him.

Guy comes forward.

Hey Guy how're you doing?

GUY   Good. Yeah. I'm good.

DAVID   Nice. Hey, why don't you tell us something about yourself?

GUY   *(Pretty nervous.)* Well my name's Guy and I'm like twenty-five and my interests include archery and car-racing. My girlfriend's name is Laura. She's sweet, really sweet. She can't be here tonight but she says hi.

DAVID   Hear that guys, Laura says hi.

MEN   Hi Laura!

GUY   Laura and I like to do special things
               together when we get time which isn't often,
               she's busy with her studies – dental hygiene
               – and I'm always working, but when we
               get a chance we like to do special things
               together.

DAVID   Like what Guy?

GUY   Oh I dunno like if it's sunny, we might
               pack a picnic lunch and hire a boat from
               one of the boat-sheds along the river, you
               know those paddle boats like swans, you
               sit inside the swan and the swan's long
               white neck sticks up in front of you while
               you paddle along the river, Laura really
               likes them, so we might hire one of those
               and paddle along the river and talk about
               things that are important to us, things we
               dream of achieving, the kind of happy life
               we imagine for ourselves, or we laugh about
               other people paddling past, their hairstyles
               or clothes, like we say to each other, 'hey
               see that woman with the frizzy hair' or
               'check out that guy's acid-wash jacket', stuff
               like that, paddling along, admiring the big
               white houses with gardens down to the
               river, the ones with their own little wharves
               and glass gazebos at the water's edge, I
               never tell Laura but sometimes I picture
               us living in one of those houses, I picture
               myself drinking a beer in the gazebo while
               gigantic insects hover around the garden in
               the hazy light of the late afternoon, Laura's
               also probably imagining what it'd be like
               to live in one of those houses, details of

how our lives would fit there, the children
we'll one day have playing on the lawn or
running down to the water's edge to wave
at passing boats, deep down we both know
we'll never really live there no matter
how kind fortune is, but it's okay, it's nice
to imagine – don't do this, just let me off
please, I know I fucked up, I was just doing
my job –

DAVID   You know this is not about you, right Guy?
I'm sorry that you and Laura will never live
in one of those huge villas by the water's
edge. I'm sorry you won't paddle together
again on a sunny afternoon with your lunch
packed in the belly of a fibre-glass swan,
but you're here because there needs to be a
bit of you know sign-off. Guy, I get it – you
were just doing your job. You beg me to let
you off lightly, to not go ahead and let my
boys who are hungry dogs smash you, but
tell me Guy how d'you think it'd look if I
didn't follow through with this? What would
the people watching my every move make
of that, huh?

Waits.

It's your turn to respond, Guy.

Waits.

Please.

Waits.

(Prompting.) Please, we can work this out,
Laura's will be home soon and –

GUY   Please, please, we can work something out.
Laura will be home soon. She'll be cleaning
the surgery at the dental hospital. She'll be

the last one there because she always works later than the others. She works so hard. Right before she switches off the banks of fluorescent-lamps like she does every night, she'll look at the powered-down machines in the empty room – machines for looking into mouths, machines for cleaning cavities, for drilling teeth, for sucking saliva – she'll see those machines shining and sparkling because she cleaned them so lovingly even though the day was long. When she switches off the lamps, the machines will glow like strange animals gathered in the moonlit surgery. She'll hear the traffic in the streets below as workers who stayed back late make their way homewards and she'll think of me and pray for my safety. She'll look forward to curling up on the sofa with me to binge watch eps of the latest long-form TV drama, all warm and cosy in each other's arms. *(Wild desperation.)* Please let me see her again. NO ONE NEEDS KNOW ABOUT THIS. We'll disappear. I promise. Please –

DAVID   It would have been better if you'd cried. *(To the men.)* Boys.

The men set upon GUY. At first he tries to laugh it off, but three of the men are on him. One smashes a bottle over his head then they lay into him. A scene of prolonged brutality. Very aggressive. It's hard to tell what's been rehearsed before and what's spontaneous. Occasionally, other fights break out among the men and it's hard to tell who's for real and who's playing. DAVID is never involved.

DAVID   We will weather the storm. The children will come. Amelia will come.

Silence.

Hope you're getting what you came for.

Checks watch.

Happiness? My picture of happiness? Okay.

The fighting begins to ease.

In the park the other day I was training with the sticks when these twins walked past. Two little girls in blue sundresses. Like yours. Like the one you're wearing now. But blue. They walked right past me holding their daddy's hands. A twin on each of his swinging arms. And the sun was dusty and golden as it shone down on them.

The violence subsides. The men are hushed. GUY lies broken. DAVID checks his watch. A man approaches the uneven bars.

The twins stood in their blue sundresses staring at me. As if they knew something about me that even I didn't know. As if they could see into my blind-spot. Their father stood between them in the dusty light. I thought the afternoon had come to a standstill. I wondered if it would ever kick into motion again. The twins. Me. The father.

The man jumps up and hangs from the bars.

He probably knew they could see right through me, probably knew they were looking into my blind-spot and reading the secret book of my soul, but he didn't care. He wasn't scared of me at all. He just waited in the sunlight for them to finish looking, until they were ready to move on.

Stillness except for the man swinging on the uneven bars.

Him. The father of those girls. He is the picture of happiness I give you today.

The man twirls and flips. He spins and spins and spins.

DAVID looks at his watch.

He's trembling.

Fade.

II.   PARIS

A departure lounge in an airport terminal.

AMELIA and ANDREW are waiting to board a flight.

AMELIA   So the taxi came and I like put on my
                smiley face and told him I was going to
                Paris. He was totally not happy.

ANDREW   What? You didn't tell him before?

AMELIA   Why should I?

                Slight pause.

                He asked like 'what the hell are you going
                to Paris for' and I said 'remember how when
                we had to like cancel our vacation and shit
                you told me to book a ticket to Paris well I
                booked it.'

ANDREW   Uh-huh.

AMELIA   He was real pissed that he didn't know and
                was like 'why didn't you tell me.' I'm all
                like, 'well what with the ups and downs in
                our relationship maybe it slipped my mind.'

                She giggles.

                Now he's telling me that he's got some kind
                of plan on *his* mind. That's what he said last
                time he phoned – 'a plan.' Bet you next he
                wants to come to Paris and meet me and I'll
                have to tell him that I'm travelling with a
                friend.

                Giggles.

                Do I have to tell him the friend's a guy?

ANDREW   Yes.

AMELIA   Oh shit he's gonna flip.

ANDREW	Sure is.
AMELIA	Can't I like tell him that I'm travelling with a girl?
ANDREW	No you can't.
AMELIA	Man is he gonna fucking flip.

They are distracted by a crying baby.

Baby sounds like a friggin' chainsaw.

ANDREW	Travel stresses babies out. They know they're far from home but no idea where, the concept of place doesn't exist for them yet, but they can still tell this isn't home, they sense its non-homeness, plus the air's not really fresh and they taste that, all these people from all these places breathing the same re-circulated air, babies taste that, plus their little ears can't handle the pressure changes in the cabin so if they've flown before, they remember and the idea of experiencing all that pain again stresses them out, they sense it coming like a cyclone twirling on the horizon, on its way to wreck your world, they know that real soon an inexplicable pain will fill their poor little heads so they wail in anticipation. The wailers are the frequent flyers.
AMELIA	Well, it's hurting my head. Why aren't we still in the lounge? Why are we at the gate if they knew it was delayed? I'd go another champers.
ANDREW	Hells yeah.
AMELIA	He was all like 'our relationship needs' and I'm like 'our relationship? I don't wanna go there.' So he asked again 'why didn't

you tell me about Paris?' I think he was screaming at me because he was drunk or just woke up. I said 'you're the one who cancelled our trip, the flights, everything, well we were on points, so I went ahead and booked it.' What did your boss want?

ANDREW I told him I'm working at home for a few days.

AMELIA You didn't tell him about Paris?

ANDREW I don't want stress right now.

She answers her ringing phone, walks away, gesticulating broadly. He walks around a bit like a guy in a cowboy film. Sits hunched. Checks his phone. AMELIA hangs up. Returns. Sits.

AMELIA Man he's really –

Her phone rings again.

I'm not answering.

She lets it ring out. They stare at the phone. It rings again.

Shit.

She lets it ring out.

Shit. I should just like turn it off.

The phone rings again.

Oh wait now it's David. I gotta get this.

She answers the phone and walks away. She listens and talks like someone in love. ANDREW snatches an occasional look at her, trying not to be too obvious about it. This goes on a bit. She, of course, knows he's snatching glances. He gets up and indicates for her to keep an eye on their bags while he looks for a kiosk or vending machine. She hangs up. Sits. Types into her phone. After a while, Andrew returns with bottled water.

So I have to go to David's.

ANDREW   What? When? Shit. Why?

AMELIA   He wants me there after Paris but he's got his 'friend' with the X-ray vision there so that kinda takes the pressure off me.

She types into screen.

This app's fucking bullshit.

Types.

That's interesting it lets me search but –

Pause.

Did he respond?

ANDREW   Who?

AMELIA   Your boss.

ANDREW   Yeah.

AMELIA   And?

ANDREW   Later.

Silence during which they are typing on their screens and sipping water.

Baby's asleep.

AMELIA   Huh?

ANDREW   The baby. In its mother's arms.

They stare.

Jesus, look. That guy just dropped his shit on the floor. Finished his burger, wiped his greasy hands then straight up dropped

37

everything – wrapper, napkin, bag – on the floor. Like a challenge. Pig.

Long silence.

AMELIA   When David's fucking me, he's always right there. Like a moon or something above me. Guys think they're there but they're not. They sweat and moan and stick themselves in me but they're not really there. They're off crossing some field somewhere, some grey fucking field or – I don't know – putting out a fire, or listing the names of their childhood football teams to stop themselves cumming, or crawling across the ceiling looking down, but they're not really there – fully present – like David is when he's fucking me.

Pause.

ANDREW   What about me?

AMELIA   What about you?

ANDREW   Am I there?

AMELIA   When?

ANDREW   When we're fucking. Am I there?

AMELIA   What do you think? Do you think you're there?

ANDREW   Sometimes.

AMELIA   Sometimes?

ANDREW   Mostly. I'm mostly there. With you.

AMELIA   You just think you're there with me. You go through the moves – touching me, making me wet, swapping positions – and a voice in your head says this is good, really good, but you're just advertising being there, like that smiling woman on that billboard over there, eating ice-cream, promising us a really good life, *heaven,* if we eat it too. Sex with you is product placement.

ANDREW   So why are we going to Paris? Why did we talk about it so much and imagine all the things we'd do there?

AMELIA   Because I like fucking you and I want to fuck you in Paris.

ANDREW   I can be there.

AMELIA   When?

ANDREW   Now. I'll be there now.

AMELIA   Where?

ANDREW   Here. I'll be there. Here. Now.

AMELIA   People can see.

ANDREW   So?

They make love. It is not rushed or self-conscious, even though people are watching. There's nothing showy or ironic about it. They are completely absorbed in each other, by turns tender and passionate. They stifle their cries when they come, and afterwards, lie wrapped in each other's arms.

AMELIA   *(Gently.)* Aren't you going to ask me?

ANDREW   What?

AMELIA   If I thought you were there with me?

ANDREW   No.

Silence. He extricates himself from her embrace, puts his clothes back on.

I felt things I can't name. Memories of
forgotten places. A taste of life without
words – not 'not speaking' but never having
spoken, never having known language,
making sounds yes, moans, grunts, growls,
even melodies, but no concept of speech
– for a moment I felt the possibility of life
without speech, like they say animals have,
but it was a mirage, and you were there,
eyes shut, inside your mirage. I knew we'd
discuss it later, that fleeting sensation at the
edge of language, that intense threshold of
being, but it would be far away now, beyond
reach. I'd fuck you over and over, suck
your mouth, get inside every part of you
looking for the feeling, but it would be gone,
unattainable, like clouds outside an airplane
window, great clusters of white, fabulous
animals, a cotton-wool sea stretching to the
horizon, utterly beautiful but impossibly
separate –

AMELIA   Unless you skydive –

ANDREW   Sorry?

AMELIA   Unless of course you skydive then –

She dresses.

– at least for a little while, you're in the
clouds, falling through that endless white.

ANDREW   When we fuck I feel like I'm trying out for a
role. Like I'm auditioning.

AMELIA   It's not like that and you know it.

*She goes and gets food from a vending machine or
kiosk. She returns, shares the food.*

ANDREW   Ta.

AMELIA   I've never done that before.

ANDREW   What?

AMELIA   Like fucked in a public like that, with all these people watching.

ANDREW   Me neither. Once we couldn't have – I don't mean 'we' couldn't have like we've suddenly achieved something that we weren't previously capable of or that we suddenly got the courage to do something we couldn't five minutes before, no, I mean once we would have been told to stop – now people just stare or pretend to look away.

AMELIA   Yeah we could have been anywhere.

ANDREW   Did I tell you about last week on the train? Those kids? There'd been this big football game which the home-side lost. The platforms and carriages were filled with drunk, devastated teenagers. Some were wrapped in flags the colours of the home-side, some had painted their faces those same colours, but all smeared now. Most of the girls wore short skirts and crop tops. The boys were muscly and smoked inside the carriage even though it's forbidden. I was listening to music on my headphones – dreamy synth stuff – imagining I was a camera observing the train, the kids, the night. There was a group of teenagers a few seats away, actually, me and the kids were the only passengers in the carriage. They were pretty smashed. Lolling about, nodding to beats on their headphones. Eyeing each other off. Suddenly one of the girls began to vomit. Really violently. A plastic bag got passed to her and she lay on

the seat trying to puke into it. Some of her
friends distanced themselves from her in
case she triggered them off too. One of her
friends kindly lifted her hair out of the way
of the puke. This real gangly girl wobbled
off on her heels, making 'eew' sounds –
disgusted – like a princess whose party was
ruined. She tottered along the aisle then
stood swaying, staring at her friends with
a strange look. Like they'd mutated into
aliens. Then possessed by a sudden urge
to establish composure, she bent down to
adjust the buckles of her silver stilettos, and
as she did so, her too-short skirt rode up
and I saw right into her naked bending ass.
It stared at me like a dilated eye.

*He looks at AMELIA. She's just gazing out into the
middle distance.*

Ever seen those clips of public gang-bangs?
They usually involve some sort of full on
humiliation of a woman in broad daylight.
The woman is pretty much always in
restraints, led on a leash through the streets
or bound in chains, yet still somehow
complicit – ravenous, *gagging for it* – even
as she's spat on, naked, hands all over
her, in every hole – all filmed guerrilla
style – like one of those hand-held Danish
films from last century – in a supermarket
or a shopping mall or the carriage of a
suburban train – and the thing is, there
are always these totally normal people in
shot, watching out the corner of their eyes,
filming on their phones or pretending to
read newspapers – those free ones they
hand out at the entrance of the station – and
– get this – nobody – at least not in the clips

I've seen – ever intervenes or expresses outrage. There's this full on tension between the juxtaposition of the explicit sex act – this brutal group fuck – with a totally banal, everyday scene. It's what gives the clips their special charge. It's porn flaunting it's ubiquitous presence, flexing its muscles, coming right out and saying hey we know you all look at this stuff on your laptops and cell-phones, well, here we are, right in your face. And at the same time, this spilling over of fantasy from the once cloistered spaces of pornography – villas, swimming pools, hotel rooms, leather seats of luxury cars, high school class rooms, dental surgeries filled with weird machines etc – signifies a shift from these traditional, increasingly outmoded, highly theatrical locations to a new cinema verité of public space. It announces an era of transgression bored with itself, transgression bored with endless fantasy, transgression seeking an *intrusion* into the real. Or does it all come down to blind market forces? The imperative to invent fresh scenarios to stimulate increasingly dulled consumers clicking away at their screens. Anyway, I was thinking about that as I listened to the synth soundtrack on my headphones and stared into the girl's asshole. If everyone was an extra in someone else's movie was there ever any chance of *not partaking* in a scene? Of not playing along? If I looked away from the bending girl's asshole, would I remain an unwitting extra in shot looking away? Like you now, Amelia. Are you even listening to me?

She won't return his gaze.

43

You're like a passenger on a train coming
home with her shopping bags when out
of the blue the other passengers restrain a
seemingly ravenous woman and handcuff
her to one of those aluminium hand rails.
Their hands go up her skirt. They tear her
shirt open. They suck her exposed breasts
and shove their cocks into her mouth until
she gags. While you pretend not to watch.
Like you pretend I don't exist.

He waits for her to say something, anything.

Nothing.

The chick looking after the puking girl
asked me if I had a tissue. I gave her a
packet. She wiped the sick one's mouth.
Soon the girl recovered enough to stand
and the group moved to another part of
the carriage away from the stink of alcohol
vomit.

He turns away.

Flag wrapped teenagers stood and swayed
on the platform like monuments to loss.
They staggered around clutching empty
vodka bottles like trophies. Some lay
crumpled, passed out beneath billboards or
vending machines. Moths circled the lamps.
I thought about you and Paris and being
real.

*Silence. She finishes whatever she's eating. Her phone
rings. She walks off and talks for a long time. Quite
still. After a while, Andrew begins to dance. A soft-
shoe shuffle. Amelia hangs up the phone. Stands apart
for a while. Watches until Andrew stops dancing.
Finally, she returns.*

AMELIA   He's flipping out.

ANDREW	You told him about going to Paris with a male friend?
AMELIA	No. Kinda. No.
ANDREW	You didn't tell him?
AMELIA	Man is he flipping the fuck out. Told you he was gonna flip.
ANDREW	Yeah.
	Pause.
	Were you watching?
AMELIA	When?
ANDREW	Just now while you were talking.
AMELIA	What? No.
ANDREW	I was dancing. Like I used to at my grandmother's. She loved the old dance films. I used to watch the tapes over and over, teach myself the steps. I just remembered. They came up from nowhere. Must've been in my body all along.
AMELIA	I didn't see. I was talking.
	Pause.
	Do it again.
	Pause.
	Do it again, knucklehead.

ANDREW dances again. AMELIA watches. He's shy at first, but gradually overcomes that. Especially because AMELIA is smiling while she watches. He crosses to her and lifts her up like Gene Kelly does to Leslie Caron in 'An American in Paris.' They dance together, very romantic, like when Gene Kelly and Leslie Caron dance to the trumpets under the fountain and in the steam. Absolutely no irony. Utterly absorbed in one another. They hold the final kiss. The light changes direction.

ANDREW   Is the announcement about us? Our flight?

They listen. (There is no announcement.)

It's impossible to understand what she's saying.

They listen.

Something about a storm.

AMELIA   No one's going to the gate. It's still closed.

ANDREW   Jesus it's hot in here. The air-con's down or something. Fuck.

AMELIA   Drink water.

ANDREW   See that guy there.

AMELIA   With the beard?

ANDREW   Him yeah. I played a guy like him once.

Pause.

Jesus, I'm tired.

AMELIA   We didn't sleep much.

ANDREW   Lot of catching up to do.

AMELIA   I woke in the night and watched you sleeping. You were tangled in the sheets, fists balled. There was this clicking noise – your jaw snapping open and shut. Like a lizard on a rock in the sun. I wondered what language you were speaking. Were you trying to tell me something? No, you were dead to the world. I played with your cock

for a while and got you hard. I put you in
my mouth and sucked you off. I wanted to
see if I could make your jaw stop clicking.
Sometimes you let out a moan – like for
instance when I put you in my mouth so
deep that I choked.

She imitates his moan.

You turned into a puppet. My moaning
puppet. But your jaw never stopped
clicking.

She imitates sucking and moaning sounds.

You didn't wake up. Not even when you
came in my mouth, jerking and twitching.
How is that even possible? I mean how can
you sleep through that? I thought maybe
you were only pretending to sleep so I
pinched you. Really hard. Here.

She points to his belly. He lifts his shirt, looks.

Is there a mark?

He's still looking.

You didn't make any noise when you came,
just your jaw snapping open and shut.

Silence. She imitates his clicking jaw.

I could have done anything to you.

Long silence punctuated by her jaw clicking.

Look at all these people – reading
newspapers, checking phones, staring at
screens, feeling overheated because the air-
conditioning broke, gazing into the halogen-
lit air like zombies. Listen to that airport
sound – heels on marble, hum of voices
like dead leaves, an announcement about

a delayed flight or a request for someone
whose name sounds ridiculous to please
come and make themselves known to staff
at a desk somewhere, the child crying, the
whirr of suitcase wheels. We're all between
places, neither here nor there. Like him –
the one playing with his fancy moustache
– where's he going? What's he left behind?
Or that cute couple there? Look how
sweetly they gaze into each other's eyes like
characters in one of those movies you used
to watch at your gran's. Look – consultants
on their way to or from smashing the
competition.

Points.

Him – the one staring at his fat fingers –
flying home after dismantling a company,
making necessary cut-backs, letting people
go, streamlining operations or whatever
the fuck – what's he thinking? Or this guy
who looks like he's been working for the
same firm forever, wondering what hotel
they've put him up in this time or what
his wife will get up to while he's away, he
looks calm and blank like everyone else but
deep down he knows he's *dead wood.* That
woman there in the twin-set and pearls –
my god – just imagine if *she* was the love of
your life. If she was the one you came home
to. The one you longed for when you were
away. The one you pick up a present for in
duty-free. Or – even better – what if *you're*
the one waiting for her at home right now?
Worried because her plane's delayed and
the special dinner you cooked is getting
spoiled. Longing for her to come home
so you can open a bottle of wine and lie

together on the sofa in baggy clothes binge watching the latest TV series. Imagine her warm in your arms in the glow of the flat-screen. Hey. She's checking you out – see? She looked at you. Maybe she recognises you. Or me. Do you think she recognises me? Does she think we look good together? That we belong together? Or are we just shapes in the room? A generic couple sitting on airport furniture, avatars generated by the programme in her brain which makes the gate lounge seem more realistic. Dumb bitch. What about him? That guy. Looking at me like he wants me. Look –

He does.

– Okay he just looked away.

They wait.

He's only pretending not to look.

ANDREW	He's just sitting there. Like everyone else.
AMELIA	Wait. Any second.

They wait.

ANDREW	He looks bored.
AMELIA	He's just pretending.

They wait.

ANDREW	I give him ten. *(He counts in silence.)*
AMELIA	There.
ANDREW	What?
AMELIA	He looked. He checked me out.
ANDREW	No.

AMELIA   Are you blind? He couldn't help himself.

ANDREW   No way.

AMELIA   Yes way. He totally eye-fucked me.

ANDREW   Uh-uh.

AMELIA   His eyes flicked over me and in that split second he stripped me bare and imagined all the things he'd do to me. He eye-fucked me the shit out of me.

ANDREW   Sure his eyes roamed round for like a second, I saw that, but he wasn't stripping you, he didn't eye-fuck you. He was checking the flight information on the monitor or just letting his eyes wander over the other people sitting around like generic shapes on the airport furniture while his brain calculated the figures related to a company he's on his way to dismantle piece by piece.

AMELIA   You have no idea. You can't see what's in front of you. Men like him look at me all the time. Like you once did. Before the endless phone-calls and emails. They look at me and imagine their future stretching in front of them – a clear, naked instant shining with impossible joy and total fulfilment. I see it flash in their eyes like I saw it in yours. He looks at me and I'm his happy future where he lacks nothing.

She points.

There! He looked again. I'm filling the hole in his life. We're supposed to snuggle up on a couch and watch endless episodes of some TV series we missed when we were busy feeding our kids or flying to distant cities to have meetings in glass buildings. We're supposed to keep each other warm and keep our children safe and make sure they've got everything they need and they're supposed to grow and watch us and learn the words we use and take their places in our world which is now their world. You have no idea what it's like to be missed by your children – missed like he is – how they miss the little things, like that song he sings them at bedtime before he switches off the light – he actually has a song about that, about switching off the light, which he sings to them just before switching off the actual light in their room, except he sings '*slitch*' instead of switch. *(Singing.) I'm so glad when my daddy hugs me tight and he slitches off the light.* Do they have any idea where he is? Those poor fucking kids? Do they know he's sitting in a transit lounge pretending not to look at me with his fuck hungry eyes? Do his children know?

Silence. Heads bowed.

ANDREW   Do you want children?

Pause.

Amelia, do you want to have children?

Two children enter and sit down. A boy of about nine and a girl of about eleven. Their passports and travel documents are hanging around their necks in those plastic pouches that children travelling without guardians wear. The boy listens to music on headphones, the girl takes out a handheld game console and plays.

AMELIA   Hey I know them.

ANDREW   What?

51

AMELIA	Yeah. They're David's kids. Why aren't they with their mother? Or someone?
ANDREW	David's children? Are you joking?
AMELIA	No. They're really his kids.
ANDREW	Go say hello then.
AMELIA	Are you serious?
ANDREW	Go on. Go say hello.
AMELIA	You cannot be serious.
ANDREW	They'd be happy to meet a familiar face. It's weird travelling alone when you're a kid. You never feel safe.
AMELIA	They're not travelling alone, they're together. Anyway, I only met them like once or twice. I've seen them playing games on the huge flat-screen David's got. Or swimming in the pool. Once I even helped rub cream into their skin before we all went for a dip but I don't know them.
ANDREW	Prove it. Prove they're his kids.
AMELIA	Man, you have got to get over this. It's stupid to be jealous of David.
ANDREW	Why do you want to go to Paris anyway? Why not get on the plane with the kids and fly straight to David?
AMELIA	Because I'm going to Paris with you. We longed for this.
ANDREW	And what's so special about Paris?

AMELIA gets up, walks around, agitated. Sits. Can hardly look at him.

Go on, tell me.

AMELIA   In Paris –

                Shakes her head..

                In Paris –

ANDREW   What?

AMELIA   We'll wake tangled in the crisp cotton
                sheets and throw the curtains open so light
                streams in and when room service knocks
                with breakfast we'll open the door wrapped
                only in towels or those fluffy white robes
                provided by the hotel, he'll lift his little
                hat when we tip him, click his heels and
                disappear down the hallway, leaving us
                bowls of steaming coffee, flaky croissants
                and buttery pastries stuffed with fruit and
                custard, after breakfast we'll shower and
                make sweet love under warm jets of water,
                we'll dress in smart yet comfortable clothes
                to visit boutiques and galleries, antique
                markets and bookshops, we'll buy each
                other perfumes which we'll spend ages
                testing before finally choosing fragrances
                which best evoke memories of being
                together in Paris, a sudden thunder storm
                will boom and flash over Paris and we'll
                pop into one of those tiny cinematheques
                tucked away in the narrow streets, we
                won't understand a thing but we'll snuggle
                up trying to remember the last time we
                watched an actual movie in an actual
                cinema, we'll fuck all afternoon back at our
                charming boutique hotel, windows flung
                open so we can see the clouds stretched
                above the garrets of Paris like some famous
                painting we always longed to see, at dusk
                we'll stroll along the Seine and drink
                champagne in a cute bar we happen upon

before dinner at a hidden bistro that the travel app recommended, we'll stumble back to the hotel half drunk and fuck each other silly until dawn breaks over Paris like an egg yolk in a glass, our love making will be incredibly passionate and utterly sincere, it will bring us closer than we ever thought possible, laughing and crying at the same time, we'll be so stupidly happy that there will be no point going on so we'll leap from the balcony of our lovely suite and splatter on the cobblestones below, hands entwined for eternity. Paris will be exactly like that. *Parfait*. Why are you here, Andrew? Why the fuck are you even here?

ANDREW   I'm here because in all those emails and phone calls you said you'd give anything to see me again. I listened to you weep when I said I couldn't come, when I explained my situation. You insisted we continue when I tried to cut it. You said I was everything, that everything depended on seeing me again. I became addicted to our phone calls, even though I knew I shouldn't answer. I hungered for your emails, even though I had to check them in secret and keep them hidden. I found myself in two realities – the confused present which had become like a picture with a stain on it, and the happy future when we'd be together again. I'd get so horny when we spoke. I'd park in a side street and jerk off while we described the things we'd do when we met. Everything I had previously wanted collapsed. I risked it all to meet you again. To be with you. And now what? When I ask about David, you look at me like I'm a plate of glass in a bus shelter waiting to be smashed. You can't stop checking your phone. You're worse than me when I was always hoping for an SMS from you. I'll find David. I'll finish the cunt. He's NOTHING.

The children look across because ANDREW raised his voice.

AMELIA   Calm down Andrew. You're disturbing people. This isn't about David.

ANDREW   Why did you even come? Is this an experiment to see how far I'll go? Some game you and David are playing?

AMELIA   Jesus.

ANDREW   I'll tell his kids how good their daddy makes you feel. Like some fucking moon above you.

AMELIA   You have to stay calm. This is not an experiment. My being here has nothing to do with David. I'm here because I want to be. Because of everything we said to each other and the things we dreamed of.

She opens her purse, takes out a compact mirror, applies lipstick, eye-liner.

Remember at the border? Lined up waiting to show our passports to the customs officials. My chest went tight and my breath was thick. I was hot all over. The hall where we stood in zigzagging lines like cattle was air-conditioned but I was burning up. I looked around the hall at the other people in the line clutching their cabin luggage, passports and duty-free shopping – YOU DON'T HAVE THE FUCKING GUTS TO TAKE ON DAVID YOU FUCKING PUSSY – all

these people held for this interval of time,
in this in-between zone – I DARE YOU
TO SMASH HIM, I FUCKING DARE
YOU – everyone's impatient to get through,
get home, wherever, some nervous about
getting through, all of us waiting to step
up and place our passports on the too-high
counter and smile at the official, hoping the
questions will be brief and kind because
we all feel guilty dealing with people in
uniform even when we know our papers are
in order and we have nothing to hide, yes of
course, we'll obey when the customs officer
instructs us to look into the lens of the black
plastic eye-ball-like device that will scan
our eyeballs for biometric information and
update our histories, I was overheating
like I was stuffed under a blanket, the
air-conditioning droned, the fluorescent
lights hummed, I wanted to ask you if you
thought it was too quiet, but I was afraid
everyone would hear me and regardless of
what language they spoke, they'd stare at
me like I was a child screaming in church
or a mobile phone ringing in a theatre, so
I held my breath and waited in line like
you and everyone else, I started thinking
what if the concept of nationality didn't
exist anymore, what if nations didn't have
borders to keep people in or out, what if
there were no lines of people waiting in
silent cattle runs, no passports, no identity
cards, no eyeball scans, Jesus fuck, I was
burning up, everything I knew began
to collapse, where I was going, where I
belonged, what was I part of, what was
mine, what I believed, who was supposed
to keep me safe, protect me, fuck, fuck,

what prevented the orderly silent line of
people from breaking down into mess
and torment, pushing, shoving, crawling
over each other to get inside – HELP ME,
SAVE ME, I WANT TO GET FREE – I
couldn't breathe like I was being crushed
in a stampede, but at the same time I felt
this incredible bond with the other people
in the line and regardless of our different
languages or the different stories our
eyeball-scans would tell, regardless of the
different futures we imagined for ourselves
and the different things we were prepared
to do to safeguard those futures, regardless
of all that, part of me wished that we'd be
delayed a bit longer in this non-place, just a
little longer, anonymous, stateless, together,
imagine, Jesus, just imagine, and right at
that moment your hand squeezed mine and
I took it as a sign that you wanted to be with
me, that the waiting had been worth it, that
we were standing on the threshold of a new
life and at that instant my heart thumped
in the thick air and the whole line breathed
in and out like a gigantic lung in a glass
and concrete box, I stopped seeing people
as projections in a dream, they weren't
generic types generated by software in my
brain to make so-called reality appear more
believable, no, they weren't extras in a film
in which we were the stars, no, each person
in that glass and concrete room shone, no
not shone, *blazed*, blazed like a sun.

Silence.

Do you understand, Andrew? Do you?

Silence.

ANDREW   That's our flight.

Silence.

Amelia, they're boarding our flight.

They collect their hand-luggage and commence boarding.

DAVID's daughter is playing her hand-held game.

His son is listening to music on his headphones. Nodding his head to the beat.

After a while he takes a harmonica from his pocket and plays 'Moon River.'

Fade.

III.   TURBULENCE

DAVID's children, AVRIL and TROY are seated in the economy class of an aeroplane. They wear disposable headphones and appear to be watching something on the fold-out screens. (We never see what's on the screen.) They appear to be watching the same thing since they react at the same time in similar ways, laughing, getting frights, 'eewing' with disgust.

TROY   (*Too loud.*) I'm hungry.

                Pause.

                (*Really loud, whacking his sister's arm.*) Avril,
                I'm hungry.

AVRIL   (*Taking off her headphones.*) Huh?

TROY   (*Still way loud.*) I said I'm hungry.

AVRIL   Take them off.

TROY   (*Loud.*) What?

                *He laughs at something on the screen, giggling like
                a hyena.*

AVRIL   Troy.

                *All the while keeping an eye on her screen, trying to
                follow what she's missing, she mimes for him to take
                his headphones off. He doesn't get it. She reaches across
                and takes his headphones off.*

TROY   Hey what did you do that for?

AVRIL   What do you want?

TROY   I'm hungry. It's been ages.

AVRIL   It'll be here soon.

TROY   Is there a chef? Why's he taking so long?

AVRIL   There's no chef. The stewards heat it up in
                the galley. They heat up all the meals.

TROY	I'm gonna have the beef.
AVRIL	I'm torn between the beef and the noodles.
TROY	I like mopping the sauce up with the bread roll. You put heaps of butter on the roll then mop up the sauce. It's the best. I love the containers the meals come in, how they fit on the tray. Peeling back the hot aluminium lid, seeing what's inside. Wish Dad would let us have airplane meals at home.
AVRIL	You know they put a special ingredient in the meals that makes you not need to go to the toilet. On long haul flights, they don't want everyone going to the toilet all the time. That's why you can't get airplane meals when you're not on airplanes. This special ingredient. Stops you farting too.
TROY	Bullcrap. Listen.

He concentrates. Tilts to the side a little.

AVRIL	What?
TROY	I farted but you didn't hear it. The seat ate it up.

AVRIL puts her headphones back on and concentrates on the screen.

AVRIL	You're gross. Eew.

He laughs, wafts the fart toward her. It stinks. She covers her face in disgust, holds her breath. Punches his arm.

You're dead when we get home Troy.

TROY puts his headphones back on.

You're so fucking dead.

Pause. She lifts his headphones to talk to him.

I'm gonna tell Dad that you were a little shit and he'll be disappointed in you.

Silence. Both absorbed in the movie again. AVRIL does up her seat belt. Puts her seat up. Gestures for TROY to remove his headphones. He eventually does.

Put your seat belt on.

TROY   No. Why.

AVRIL   Don't you hear the announcement? Don't you see how the movie's frozen so the flight attendant can make the announcement? We're flying through unexpected turbulence so we have to put our seats up, fasten our seat-belts and fold away our tray-tables.

TROY   Turbulence. What's turbulence?

AVRIL   You know what turbulence is, dickhead. Means the plane will shake.

TROY   Are we going to crash?

AVRIL   No. It's just – it means the air outside is unpredictable, like if we're going through clouds and there's electricity.

TROY   Are you sure it's not terrorists? I saw some guys who looked like terrorists. Maybe they made knives from soft-drink cans and cut the flight attendants and took over the cockpit. And that's why we're not getting our meals. The flight attendants can't heat them up if the terrorists got them.

The first jolt of turbulence.

Whoa.

Turbulence.

My tummy went in my mouth. Like at Disney World.

More turbulence.

Shit.

AVRIL	Tighten your seatbelt Troy. Hold on.

Severe turbulence. The children hold on.

TROY	Avril.

Turbulence.

Avril. I'm scared.

All the while turbulence under the following.

It's bad. Avril? It's pretty bad, isn't it?

AVRIL	Just ride it out. Watch the movie.
TROY	Can't. It's all shaky.
AVRIL	Just hold on.
TROY	Out the window – purple, flashing.
AVRIL	That's lightning. It's how lightning looks up close. We're inside the storm.
TROY	I'm scared.

AVRIL holds his hand. They close their eyes and ride it out.

Avril, I'm scared.

Silence. Shaking. Intense, terrifying turbulence.

They ride it out.

It settles down.

AVRIL	You can open your eyes, Troy. All clear.

He does.

Look, clouds. Like castles. Oh look – a rhinoceros.

He looks.

TROY
It's not a rhino. It's an elephant. Can't you see the trunk? It's a huge elephant and there's a man on it. With a big, torn flag.

They look out the porthole.

I need to go to the toilet.

AVRIL
You gotta wait until they turn off the seat-belt sign.

TROY
I need to go now.

AVRIL
Hold it in.

TROY stares at the seat-belt sign, waiting.

TROY
I'm gonna piss myself if I don't go.

They watch their films, laugh in unison.

AVRIL
Awww –

They laugh and react as if they're watching someone falling over repeatedly or getting beaten up in a funny way. Seat-belt finally signs turns off.

That's it you can go now.

TROY undoes his seatbelt and disappears down the aisle to the loo. Watching the film, AVRIL giggles to herself. She becomes deeply affected by the movie, increasingly distressed. She sheds silent tears. TROY returns. Sits. Puts headphones on.

TROY
There was pee on the floor.

AVRIL
Eew.

TROY
A puddle.

AVRIL	Gross.
TROY	What happened?
AVRIL	*(Still watching.)* She came back but everyone was gone. She searched the house but couldn't find anyone. Her room was all messed up. Kenny was gone. Pages were torn from her diary. She was angry with Paul and Lizzie for betraying her whereabouts. And really scared for Kenny. She's driving around looking for him. There's a storm coming. And he's too small to survive out there on his own.

They both watch intensely. Very concentrated. After a while, AVRIL gets up.

AVRIL	I'm going to the loo.
TROY	Wipe the seat first.
AVRIL	Eeew.

She disappears down the aisle. TROY stares at the movie. After a while, he takes some coloured crayons and paper from one of those fun-packs that they give to kids when they fly. He folds his tray-table down and draws. He keeps an eye on the screen while he makes several drawings. The seat-belt sign goes on. A jolt or two of turbulence. TROY tries to keep drawing. The turbulence gets nasty. TROY is terrified. The more terrified he is, the more he tries to draw. Eventually, the turbulence subsides. It's calm. The fasten-seat belt sign is turned off. AVRIL returns. Sits.

AVRIL	Wow, that was full on. I was sitting on the loo. I'd been waiting for a heaps long time, looking out the window at the clouds, this weird pink. Eventually the loo was free and I was on the toilet when the seat-belt sign went on and the plane started shaking.

I had to try and finish what I was doing without peeing on myself, it was fully hard to wash my hands with the plane jumping around, I got chucked around against the walls. When I opened the door, a flight attendant lady was there, she helped me to a spare seat and did my seat belt up. Were you scared?

Pause.

(Meaning the movie.) What happened?

TROY	She found Kenny –
AVRIL	I saw that.
TROY	She found Kenny in this barn. He was all wet and shivering. Shit scared. Like a little pussy. They cried tears of relief when they met. Then the roof smashed in. The leg of one of the machines smashed through the roof. This black metal eye-ball thing on a long retractable metal arm searched the barn for them. They hid under a section of collapsed roof. Kenny was whimpering and you could tell he wanted to howl like a bitch but she kept her hand over his mouth and held him tight until the machine was gone and it was safe again. Those machines were gathered in the moonlight like animals waiting. The distant city lights shone. She wants to get there, meet Kevin –
AVRIL	Hold on, Kevin?
TROY	Yeah Kevin can you believe it?
AVRIL	Wait, who's Kevin?
TROY	Kevin. You know Kevin. Wait you don't know Kevin? He's the one they're looking

for. The key to their future. You remember – she used to work with him in the lab and everyone thought he was really evil, one of the synthetics, but he ended up being the only one who can help them, if she can find him. Shit, he might even be the father Kenny's never had. You seriously don't know Kevin? Anyway, the machines are just waiting in the moonlight. The light's weird and there's this flashing orb thing taking up half the sky. It's full of energy and shooting out lightning bolts. I don't get it. I mean why are they waiting. Why not keep looking?

AVRIL   What're you drawing?

TROY   Just pictures.

AVRIL   Can I see?

She looks at a picture.

TROY   That's the machines.

Another.

This one got messed up by the turbulence.

Another.

That's Dad and Kane fighting.

Another.

That's the storm. That's our plane. That's you looking out the window.

Pause.

AVRIL   What's this one? It's really special.

Pause.

What is it, Troy?

TROY	Nothing.
AVRIL	You can tell me. It's okay.
TROY	The plane was rattling and I wanted you to come back and you kept not coming back.

Pause.

It's what death looks like.

Pause.

AVRIL	Like a sun... A black sun...

He nods.

What's that, Troy? Is that a horse? Is a horse riding though the sun? Who's that? Who's the rider?

Turbulence. Sudden and aggressive. The children scramble to put their seat-belts on and their tray tables up. The seat-belt sign turns on. The plane drops and lurches and judders. It's terrifying.

Close your eyes. Picture somewhere beautiful.

They do.

Imagine your favourite place... The most beautiful place in the world... You and I are there together... We're walking... Walking and looking at the beautiful things... The whole world turns blue... It's lovely... It's perfect...

The plane rattles.

They hold on.

Fade.

IV.   THE WRECKAGE

DAVID, alone in the concrete room, hooked up to life support. Maybe some of the apparatus from Act I are still there – the rings, pommel horse, parallel bars – now in ruin. DAVID speaks, but his words are not comprehensible or especially audible. After a while, he tries to crane his neck. His movement is severely limited. He tries to call, can't muster much voice. He tries and fails repeatedly. It's extremely frustrating. After some time KANE turns up, looking the worse for wear. He fiddles around DAVID's neck and face, connecting something.

KANE   Yeah yeah, hold on.

DAVID   *(Inaudible.)*

KANE   Hold your horses. I'm on it.

DAVID   *(Inaudible.)*

KANE   If you keep moving your head around, I'll never get it connected.

                As KANE backs away from DAVID, he spools a black wire which he connects to a machine on a desk in the far corner of the room. He fiddles with some knobs. Finally, DAVID's amplified voice can be heard. Extra loud. His voice is very weak. It's an effort to speak.

DAVID   Kane you fucking loser.

                DAVID clears his throat.

                Right – where were we?

                Silence.

                They told me I was everything. Bounced me on their knees. Told me I could be whatever I wanted. They said the world is yours.

                Silence.

                I like what you've done with your hair by the way. Suits you.

Silence.

I missed you. I'm glad you're back. It's nice to be looked at by you.

He laughs, but it hurts.

Kane told me what happened. I don't believe him. It happened to someone else. Not me.

Silence.

A character called David had a kingdom. Now it's gone. Now is mess and torment. His soldiers are gone. Lovers gone. Family gone. Top of the game but he got smashed.

Silence.

They beat me until I didn't know my name anymore. I woke up like this. Dismantled.

Silence.

Yeah.

Silence.

Excuse me. Just a sec. *(To KANE, quietly.)* Kane can you like you know.

KANE brings water. Feeds him like a child feeding an injured bird. Mops up dribble.

Everything else comes through the straws. I require water to speak. Or my mouth turns to dust.

KANE finishes.

Thanks Kaney. Kane's good to me.

Silence.

Why are you still here, Kane?

Silence.

Got this constant urge to check my watch.
Can't of course. Can't even tilt wrist, turn
head and check. Kane says I used to do it all
the time. That I made a habit of it.

*KANE brings DAVID's old watch from the table and
cleans the face. He attaches the watch to DAVID's wrist.
DAVID tries to look at it. It's hopeless. Exhausting. This
goes on for way too long. It's painful.*

*A woman in her late 20s, LAURA, enters and watches
DAVID. She wears a cotton sundress. KANE smiles
when he sees her. She raises a finger to her lips to
indicate shush. DAVID does not see her. She watches
him failing to look at his watch.*

The storm hit us hard but we weathered it.
No one will survive the storm that's coming.
Seven trumpets will sound an awakening.
The door will open. Everyone stampedes,
clawing, shoving, crawling over each other
to get in. We hold onto our loved ones,
but it's hopeless. They disappear in the
crowd. Gone. The tunnel's too crowded, too
narrow. Men and woman with the faces of
beasts. Beasts with human heads. Mouths
spraying saliva. *Is this death and hell a person?*
Yes. *What is he?* He is a rider. *What rider?*
A pale rider. *And his name is what?* Death,
his name is death. *What do you do when you
die?* Nothing. *Wrong. What's the sound your
body makes when it dies?* No sound. It doesn't
make any sound. *WHAT'S THE SOUND?*
RATTLE. IT RATTLES. *THAT'S THE
SOUND.* I WANT TO SEE DADDY'S
FACE THE SUN IS DARK THE STARS
FALL LET ME SEE HIS GLORIOUS
FACE –

KANE unplugs DAVID's microphone. DAVID's breathing is wracked. Like a stuck pig, or someone trapped in a stampede. Spent, he falls silent. Closes his eyes. He might be sleeping or maybe his eyes are just closed.

KANE   *(Quietly to LAURA.)* He's always like this now. Talks to thin air. He wanted to be louder so I got him the microphone. Thought it'd make him happy but he gets all stressed out. I have to unplug him, let him rest or he'd wear himself out.

Pause.

Say something if you want. He's listening.

Silence during which LAURA takes a compact mirror from her handbag. Looks at herself.

LAURA   *(To DAVID.)* I wanted to see if I was different, if seeing you had changed me. Thought I'd be angrier, really shaking, trembling voice. If anything I feel calm. I imagined this day over and over. I'd be sucking the saliva out of a patient's mouth with one of those long bendy straws while the dentist drilled into a root canal, and I'd stare into the dark pink hole of the mouth. The patient's mouth was fixed open in a silent scream and I imagined it was your face. The pit of your face. Eyes helpless. Staring. I could do anything to you.

Silence.

I don't believe the end is coming. I don't believe in the coming storm. There's no grand finale, no day of wrath. Forget your stupid trumpets. Maybe the end happened already and we missed it. Maybe it already happened and things are just as they were –

71

sad or happy, atrocious or blessed, beyond repair. Like you. Lying there with your machines which breathe for you and drip nutrients down tubes into your insides and suck the waste out of you. I could shut you down like –

She clicks her fingers.

This is the world to come. You cunt.

Silence.

When we'd had a really good day, done something special, just the two of us, like gone paddling on a lake, or picked wildflowers in the mountains, blueberries which stained our fingers, or perhaps we'd just taken it easy, breakfast at our favourite spot, a movie in the afternoon, made love, fallen asleep tangled in each other, well, after one of those good days, Guy would always say, thanks for today, so polite, lying beside me in our bed, *thanks for today,* like a little boy. Guy didn't know I was pregnant when they – when *you* – killed him. It must sound pretty corny me saying that he was killed without knowing he was going to be a father, like a scene from one of those films you watch on an aeroplane during a long-haul flight. I feel corny saying it but that doesn't change a thing. I was pregnant with our first child. Our son. His name's Michael and –

She cracks up.

I'm sorry.

She's laughing like she might wet herself.

I just need a sec.

Trying to gain composure.

Wait.

She calms down.

I have a son and his name is Michael.

Laughs silently.

(Quietly.) His name's Michael and he's
fifteen months old. Just starting to walk
around without wobbling too much.
Starting to talk too. Mostly nonsense. He
jabbers away about everything and I act
like I understand him. When I look into his
eyes, I see galaxies swirling. One day, I'll
have to tell him about his dad. About what
happened. I don't want him knowing about
you. I don't want you cast as the minotaur
in the maze of his dreams, the beast he
thinks he has to get strong enough to kill.
You're not worth it. You're nothing.

Breaks into laughter again.

'You're not worth it. You're NOTHING.'

Laughter.

Jesus, I sound like a woman in a movie on
an aeroplane. A cliché.

She laughs at herself.

If I say I forgive you, I'm that woman. If I
torture you and make you suffer for what
you did, I'm still that woman. Even if I walk
away, I'm her. Maybe I'm just making this
up. Maybe there is no Michael. No galaxies
in his eyes. I'm tired of fables. I want to
say goodnight. Now we've met, I'll say
goodnight. I'll leave you to your dreams.

73

Your splendid, monstrous dreams. Leave you to fill the world with words. Goodnight.

She goes and whispers to KANE who re-connects DAVID's mic. LAURA stands where DAVID can't see her. Very still. After a long silence –

DAVID It's foggy. I'm walking through the forest toward the silver house. The air stinks of gasoline. Must've got lost. Scratches on my arms, bloody knees. I call my brother's name but my voice echoes through the gullies. The stables are empty, the horses have fled. The doors and windows of our silver house are flung open. A curtain flaps, as if a breeze is blowing from inside out. It frightens me. My parents are not snuggled up on the sofa. My brother isn't in his room playing with his things. Everyone left in a hurry. I'm alone. A shard of blue glass is lying on the table. It's warm. I hold it to my eye and look at the sun streaming through the window. The world turns blue.

Pause.

This is the picture of happiness I give you today.

Pause.

Hope you got what you came for.

LAURA exits.

DAVID's eyes remain closed. It's hard to tell if he's resting or sleeping. Or dead. One by one, KANE powers down the machines that David is hooked up to. He disconnects the machines from the power-source and wheels DAVID out. The stage is empty for some moments.

A distant vibration is heard. Like something being torn or flying away.

AVRIL and TROY enter. They are playing with the sticks that DAVID wielded in Act I. They perform gentle exercises with the sticks or stare into space. Maybe they play on any left over gymnastic equipment.

TROY has the chess piece – the king – that DAVID had. He balances it on his palm.

AVRIL   Give me that.

TROY closes his fist over the chess piece. Avril holds out her hand. Eventually, TROY hands it over. AVRIL throws it as hard as she can against the wall. It shatters into a million pieces.

AMELIA enters. She carries a bucket (probably the same one that KANE used in Act I) and some other utensils, string etc.

AMELIA   There you are. I was looking for you everywhere.

AVRIL   We're just here.

The kids join AMELIA and they work away at something together.

AMELIA   Thread that through there. Good. Yeah, like that. Hey, that's looking good.

They use the sticks and the string to assemble one of those things for making giant bubbles. Amelia puts some detergent in the bucket and the children dip their contraption into the detergent. They take turns at making giant bubbles.

The light changes direction without becoming darker. Amelia watches the children, the bubbles.

ANDREW enters and watches for a while.

ANDREW   *(To AMELIA.)* It's time to go.

AMELIA   Give them a few more moments.

              Bubbles.

              Lights fade.

EVERY BREATH

Every Breath was first produced by Belvoir at Belvoir Street Theatre, Sydney, on 28 March 2012, with the following cast:

LEO	John Howard
CHRIS	Shelly Lauman
OLIVIA	Eloise Mignon
LYDIA	Angie Miliken
OLIVER	Dylan Young

Directed by Benedict Andrews
Set and costume design by Alice Babidge
Lighting design by Nick Schlieper
Original music by Oren Ambarchi
Sound design by Luke Smiles

Characters

CHRIS, 18

LYDIA, 44

LEO, 52

OLIVIA, 16

OLIVER, 16

CHRIS.

Wearing the uniform of a security guard.

Stands watch.

*

CHRIS, LYDIA.

LYDIA	Don't you get lonely out here?
CHRIS	Not really. No.
LYDIA	I'd get lonely. Out here with my thoughts. All that time to fill.
	Pause.
	It's a beautiful evening.
CHRIS	Yes.
	Silence.
LYDIA	Sunset. The clouds reflected in the pool.
	Slight pause.
	Will you join us tonight for dinner? You've been with us for weeks and we've never eaten together.
CHRIS	I'm not really supposed to.
LYDIA	We won't tell.
CHRIS	I can't. Really.
LYDIA	Please. It's the kids' birthday, they'd love it if you joined us.
	Pause.
	We'd all love to get to know you better.

Pause.

We hardly know you.

Pause.

C'mon. We won't bite.

*

CHRIS, OLIVIA, OLIVER, LEO, LYDIA.

The twins' birthday dinner.

CHRIS   *(To LEO.)* Really. I couldn't fit another thing in. It was great though. Really great.

OLIVIA   You'd never eaten artichokes before?

Slight pause.

We love them. Dipping them in the butter. Scraping their flesh out along our teeth.

CHRIS   Yeah. No. They're really tasty. Never had caviar before either.

OLIVIA   Isn't it something? How it pops in your mouth.

OLIVER   Dad gets it for us every birthday.

LEO   So – *(Raising his glass.)* To sturgeon roe which pop in the mouth, to being a virgin artichoke dipper and to – Oliver, top Chris up.

CHRIS   I really shouldn't have more. I'm working.

LYDIA   You'll be fine. If you fall in the pool, we'll fish you out.

OLIVER fills CHRIS' empty champagne glass.

They raise their glasses.

LEO	To our two ripe olives – Oliver and Olivia – Happy Birthday darlings!
	They drink.
	Sixteen very full years ago you came into our lives. Feels like yesterday. Happiest day of our lives.
LYDIA	*(Laughing.)* Speak for yourself. *(To CHRIS.)* Forty-eight hours of labour. At home. Splashing around in an inflatable pool. Screaming. No drugs. Agony. But worth every second. It was right there. You two were born right over there where the pot plant is standing now.
OLIVIA	*(To CHRIS.)* Guess who was first?
CHRIS	I dunno. Oliver.
OLIVIA	Nup.
OLIVER	Olivia's thirty-eight minutes older than me and never lets me forget it.
OLIVIA	That's right, buster.
LEO	And *(He raises his glass.)* To Chris. Welcome.
	Everyone except CHRIS raises their glasses.
	We sleep much better at night with you out there. Watching over us.
LYDIA	To Chris. Our guardian angel.
OLIVIA & OLIVER	Our guardian angel.
	They drink.
	CHRIS blushes.

*

CHRIS.

Stands watch.

Cracks knuckles.

*

CHRIS, LEO.

LEO   I can't sleep. Overdid it with the pork belly.

               Slight pause.

               Beautiful night. So clear.

               Pause.

               Know what those ones are called?

               (Points.) There.

               They look at the stars.

CHRIS   I never learnt the names.

LEO   Guess.

CHRIS   I dunno.

LEO   What do you see? Think.

CHRIS   I dunno. Maybe – like – a lion.

LEO   It's Orion. The hunter. That's his sword.
               See. There. And that's a *lion* he's just
               skinned hanging over his arm.

               Pause.

               What do you like to do when you're not
               working Chris?

CHRIS   Like, what d'you mean?

LEO	Do you have a hobby, something special you enjoy doing?
CHRIS	Not really. I like sport I guess. Watching sport. And going for drives. Just driving out of town and finding new places. That's relaxing. Just driving.
LEO	With your girlfriend?
CHRIS	Nah. I go driving alone. Don't really have a girlfriend.

Pause.

It's hard with the work. I'm only home for a few hours during the day. And I mostly sleep. Then before I know it, I'm getting ready to come back.

LEO	Been doing this long? Security.

Pause.

I know – all these questions. Sorry.

CHRIS	No. It's fine. I just should, you know, be keeping an eye on things.
LEO	Sure. Sure. I'll let you be.

Slight pause.

You know before the threat, I'd never have believed that we'd have someone like you standing out by the pool at night. Checking that our windows and doors are properly locked. Listening for movement in the shadows.

Pause.

I still find it hard to believe. But I'm glad you're here Chris. We're all glad you're here.

Look.

He points to the sky.

A shooting star. Did you see it?

*

CHRIS.

Watching.

Fights off sleep. Pinches self etc.

Time passes.

Dawn.

*

CHRIS.

Reading.

OLIVER enters, unseen. Watches CHRIS reading.

OLIVER	What're you reading?
CHRIS	*(Hiding cover.)* Nothing.
OLIVER	Nothing? Looks more like a book. Lemme see.

CHRIS keeps it hidden.

Are you allowed to read at work?

Beat.

Aren't you meant to be like keeping an eye out. C'mon. Show me.

CHRIS shows.

Knew it.

Slight pause.

Read him before?

CHRIS   No. This is the first one.

OLIVER   And? What do you think?

Pause.

It's not one of his best. The surrealism is too up front. The poet's 'frenzied voice' too loud. Show-off-y. The metaphors are startling, sure they – what? – they grab you, but he's yet to find genuine clarity – the diamond clarity of his best work. That's to come. In this one, he over-says things. The words clamour for attention. It's – I dunno – *overdone.*

CHRIS   I've never read anything like it.

*

CHRIS.

Watching.

Smokes.

OLIVIA enters.

OLIVIA   Can I have one?

CHRIS   What?

OLIVIA   A smoke. One of your smokes.

CHRIS   I don't think so.

OLIVIA   Why not?

CHRIS   Your parents, they wouldn't like it.

OLIVIA	I won't tell. C'mon. They're fast asleep. Please.
	CHRIS thinks about it. Looks around to make sure they're alone. Gives her one.
	She puts it in her mouth, leans in for a light.
	CHRIS tries. The lighter won't light. It just sparks.
	Eventually, it lights.
	Thanks tiger.
	Silence.
	They smoke.
CHRIS	Nice night.
OLIVIA	Huh?
CHRIS	Nice night. Real clear. All the stars.
OLIVIA	Yeah. Right. Nice.
	Pause.
	So. Do you like it here?
CHRIS	Yeah. It's fine I guess. It's nice.
OLIVIA	And as far as people watching goes, are we good people to watch?
CHRIS	Yeah. Sure.
	Pause.
	Well. I'm not exactly watching you. More like *watching out* for you. Keeping an eye on things.
OLIVIA	And if things go bad then what?
	Beat.
	Like if trouble arrives, what would you do?

CHRIS   Well. There are procedures I follow.
             Procedures I've been trained in.

             Pause.

             In case of an eventuality.

OLIVIA   So if an eventuality eventuates, would you
             like *take them on*? Could you take them
             down? Single-handedly?

             Slight pause.

CHRIS   Well –

OLIVIA   I saw you watching me.

             Pause.

             Last night. I saw you watching me.

CHRIS   It's my job to watch you.

OLIVIA   You just said it was more like 'watching
             out' not 'watching'. I saw you looking in,
             watching me.

             Pause.

             Last night when everyone had gone to bed.
             Remember? After the party.

             Pause.

             Did you think I didn't know you were there?
             On the other side of the glass? Watching.

             Slight pause.

             I was thinking about you while I touched
             myself. My guardian angel watching from
             the shadows. When I came – remember?
             – I was lying on my belly, the fingers I'd
             been sucking to make wet were between
             my thighs – you remember – when I

came I thought of you standing out here in your uniform under the stars, the scent of frangipani and chlorine in the air, your cock sticking out through the zipper. Kiss me.

Beat.

Kiss me knucklehead. Kiss me. No-one's watching.

A prolonged kiss.

*

CHRIS, LEO.

LEO   Oliver told me.

Pause.

It's fine. Really. Don't worry.

Slight pause.

Actually, I'm flattered it was one of mine.

Beat.

Your first one? Or what?

CHRIS   I –

LEO   Anyway. Doesn't matter. You chose an early one to start with. I like the early ones. Even now. But – well, they're not to every one's taste. Bit *full on.*

Slight pause.

Most people prefer later ones – from around when I turned forty – the ones described as luminous.

CHRIS	I'm not much of a reader. I'd never heard of you. Sorry.
LEO	No need to apologise. It's refreshing to talk to you, Chris. Most people think they know me inside out. Think they know who I am because of stories of mine they read. They mistake my characters' thoughts for mine. They assume privileged access to the 'secret book of my soul.' Even Lydia. The kids. They confuse our lives and my books. Yes, sometimes it's tricky to know what's producing what. Is life generating the books, or the books, the life? All that ballyhoo. The boring answer is that it's probably a bit of both. Do you know what a Möbius Strip is Chris? It's a surface with only one side and only one boundary. Imagine taking a strip of paper giving it a half-twist then joining both ends together to form a loop. You'd have a Möbius Strip. It appears to have two sides, but in fact it has only one continuous side. Now imagine an ant crawling along the length of the strip. It can crawl until it has reached its starting point again, can traverse every part of the strip without ever crossing an edge. Do you see? The ant is like the writer crawling along both so-called sides of art and life simultaneously. People think they know me. They think they see into me. Into my blind-spot, but it's always themselves they see. It's different with you Chris. I'm relieved you don't know my work. That you've only read a story or two. That you don't know my poems by heart. That you've never sat through one of my plays. You needn't feel ashamed about it. You're a godsend.

Silence.

They stare into the night.

*

CHRIS.

Watching.

A voice crackles on the walkie-talkie.

CHRIS *talks into the walkie talkie. It's impossible to decipher the conversation.*

*

CHRIS, OLIVIA.

CHRIS *kisses* OLIVIA *between her thighs.*

OLIVIA   Slower. Slower Chris.

                Like that yes.

                Look at me.

                Look at me while you taste me.

                Look at me.

                CHRIS *does.*

                Yes. Like that.

                Your eyes.

*

CHRIS, LYDIA.

LYDIA climbs out of the pool.

LYDIA   I love swimming at night. Empties me. I
like it best when I'm alone. It's the only
time I really relax. Do my laps undisturbed.
Float on my back and get lost in the stars.
On nights like this. The air thick with
frangipani and jasmine. All alone. Leo's at
a meeting for one of the boards he's on. The
kids have got a party. I said we shouldn't
let them go but they begged and begged
and Leo's convinced it's safe – that no-one
would try anything there. I'm relieved to
be alone, to swim under the stars in peace.
Well, not alone. You're here. I know *that*.
But you say so little, I may as well be alone.
I like how you watch me. I felt your eyes on
me in the pool. You make me feel safe.

Slight pause.

Why don't you lie down here beside me
Chris. On the towel. There's room on the
towel. Don't be nervous. I don't bite. Lie
down beside me, we'll look at the stars.

CHRIS lies down beside her.

Closer.

CHRIS moves a little closer.

Aren't they beautiful. Leo knows their
names. When we first met – when we were
wild for each other – we'd lie like this,
under the stars, and he'd name them, tell
me the stories up there. Long time since
we did that. Living with Leo is like living
with a black hole. He sucks in everything.
Our lives. There is no Leo. There's only

93

pages to be filled. He's not here. Really here. There's always some other *scene* going on in his head and he's imagining what the people are doing there, what they say to each other. He'd say he eavesdrops, that he merely observes the scene, listens, writes the transcript. He's too full – of scenarios, metaphors, *words*.

Silence.

I miss being with someone. Lying together, saying nothing, the entire world breathing through us. Like this. Together.

Silence.

I've felt better since you've been here Chris.

She undoes CHRIS' belt.

CHRIS   Wait –

She takes down CHRIS' trousers.

I –

LYDIA   It's okay. I know.

She spreads CHRIS' legs.

Her head disappears between CHRIS' legs.

Silence. CHRIS gazes into the stars.

*

CHRIS, OLIVER.

OLIVER practises the trombone. Bach, Cello Suite 1.

CHRIS listens.

CHRIS   Nice.

OLIVER plays.

OLIVER   Dad used to play the trombone. He was really into – you know like – *jazz*. They had to do compulsory service in the reserves back then and he hated it. Fucking hated it. He told them he was a pacifist, but it didn't wash. Took his trombone with him – like some 'appendage' – to the first training camp, thinking he'd be able to practise his bebop. On like his third morning there, he got woken up along with the rest of his squad by some guys – big, muscly soldier guys – bursting into the dorm screaming 'who's the faggot with the horn?' And, sitting on the edge of his bunk in his army issue underwear, he confessed that the horn was his and handed it over when they demanded it and watched as they each took turns to piss into the bell. They ordered him to leave it home next time. And he never played trombone again. But you know that right? You read it in one of his books.

    OLIVER practises.

*

CHRIS, OLIVER, OLIVIA.

Twins swimming.

CHRIS watches.

OLIVER   *(To CHRIS.)* It's great. Come in.

CHRIS   Haven't got swimmers.

OLIVIA   So? Swim in your daks.

OLIVER   Or nude.

OLIVER removes his swimmers.

Go on.

(To OLIVIA.) You too.

After a slight pause, she does.

Silence.

C'mon. Get in you pussy.

CHRIS is trembling.

Check it out – shaking like a pussy.

CHRIS is shaking. Tries to control it.

Some security guard.

CHRIS shivers.

OLIVIA   *(To OLIVER.)* Stop it.

OLIVER   *(Splashing CHRIS.)* Pussy! Pussy! Pussy!

OLIVIA climbs from the pool and holds CHRIS.

OLIVIA   *(To CHRIS.)* Chris it's okay. Hey it's okay. Everything's fine, Chris.

(To OLIVER.) Fuckhead.

*

CHRIS, OLIVIA.

Making out. Her hand inside CHRIS' trousers.

OLIVIA   Think we look the same?

CHRIS   Who?

OLIVIA   You know. Me and Oliver.

CHRIS   Yeah. Sure. Like –

OLIVIA   Mirrors. Right? Do you have any idea what
           it's like to walk around with this *living,*
           breathing mirror beside you? Someone who
           always says what you're thinking, just when
           the thought pops into your head? Who likes
           what you like and wants what you want?
           Can you imagine what it's like to live with
           a constant reminder of your absolute lack
           of singularity? I want so very much to be
           different, Chris.

           Silence.

           I'm jealous. Of you.

           Slight pause.

           Show me how being different feels.

           Kissing CHRIS hungrily.

           Make me different Chris.

                           *

CHRIS, OLIVER.

OLIVER   I can't sleep.

           Silence.

           You thirsty? Can I get you something? Like
           a drink or something? A coffee? Or like a
           Coke? To help, you know, stay up.

           Slight pause.

           Is it hard staying up all night? I mean you
           wouldn't want to like nod off and something
           happen. I mean imagine you like fall asleep
           and some shit goes down. You wake up
           all confused, not knowing where you are.

You notice that like a door that shouldn't
be open is open or a plate glass window is
smashed. So you go in and check and we're
like all dead. *Slaughtered.* Mum and Dad are
all chopped and bloody in the bed. I'm like
hanging from the ceiling or something. And
when you get to Olivia's room, she's been
raped and stabbed, all bloody too. Maybe
she's like not really even dead yet and you
try to – I know about you and my sister.

꙳

CHRIS.

Watching.

Hears something or someone moving in the shadows.

Listens.

*

CHRIS, LEO.

Both with cans of beer.

LEO	What about when you finished school? Ever think about continuing your studies? Going to uni?
CHRIS	I've just never known what I want to do. You know, like what to follow.
LEO	Did you have any subjects that you especially loved most at school?
CHRIS	Dunno, I was pretty quiet.
LEO	That doesn't mean that you didn't have a favourite subject. What got you excited?

CHRIS	History, I guess. I liked learning about history. How things changed.

LEO finishes his beer. Crushes the can. Chucks it in the pool.

CHRIS watches him. Does the same.

LEO	Another one?
CHRIS	I shouldn't. Getting a bit pissed.
LEO	*(Throwing him a can.)* Go on – I'm having one.

Slight pause. CHRIS cracks the can.

(Cracking a new one.) When I was your age, maybe a bit younger, just starting at university, my BA, I was living in a share house – I know typical – and I was smoking a fair bit of weed. Do you smoke dope? My kids do. Anyway, I'd get high and work on my stories or poems, mostly garbage, the kindling that gets the fire going. Well, one story I wrote back then kinda reminds me of you, the character is a bit of a blank – no offence – like you. Doesn't really know what he wants to. That in between age, between school and whatever. Doesn't do much, sleeps in, drinks coffee, plays pinball, rides around on his bike, drops in on friends, girlfriends, gets laid. One summer, one typically *sticky* summer, he's walking along the street kicking a stone or something when he finds an empty glass bottle in the gutter or stuck in a drain. An old fashioned soft drink bottle – you know with the contoured edges – and inside the bottle is a note. He smashes the bottle, reads the note and it's like some kind of zen koan, you know like 'Wave

and Sea are One.' The message is printed
in fire-engine red and below the message,
it reads 'LOVE CO   CO' – like Chanel
but weirdly spaced. C O space space space
C O. Anyway to cut a long, preposterous
story short, he keeps finding these bottles
in all sorts of weird places, bobbing in the
chlorinated waters of the public pool, behind
the pinball parlour, in the overgrown garden
of the scruffy share-house etc and he invents
all sorts of special ways to open the bottles
like putting one on a fence and shooting it
with ball-bearings from a toy Uzi 9mm pistol
or slicing it with a special crystal blade so it
collapses into psychedelic patterns. Stuff like
that. He becomes addicted to the messages
in the bottles – riddles, aphorisms, erotic
fantasies, puzzles, essays, prayers, bad jokes,
even a recipe for nettle soup – all signed
with love from this mysterious Co Co. This
Co Co who seems to understand him so
well. He sees less and less of his friends,
is increasingly obsessed with his bottles.
His friends think he's lost his mind but do
nothing to help him. Well eventually in
one of the bottles, there's a map – to some
island across the seas – and he somehow gets
hold of a boat, packs a few provisions and
precious things in a backpack and rows off
into the blue yonder. After some time at sea
following the map, a bump appears on the
horizon, an island shaped, yes, like a breast –
just like on the map – he drags his boat onto
the shore and –

CHRIS' walkie-talkie crackles.

An indecipherable voice.

CHRIS   I should –

LEO   Ignore it.

CHRIS ignores it.

Static and crackles under the following.

LEO   – crossing the beach, he realises that the red sands are really particles of ground fibre-glass and when he begins to climb the breast-shaped mountain, he realises it too is fibre-glass. A hollow construction. There are nettles growing all over the surface – impossible I know, don't ask me why, always had a thing for nettles, they're beautiful don't you think? – anyway eventually, up near the nipple, he finds a hatch and climbs down a ladder into a concrete bunker, all very James Bond, no one there, it's *devoid of people* but there are thousands upon thousands of empty Coke bottles and thousands upon thousands of tiny piles of message shaped paper and there's a desk and a chair and he sits and on the worn desktop is a stack of red pens and a red ink pad and a stamp with 'CO   CO' on it and only now that he's sitting at the desk and his boat's been swept out to sea because in his haste to get on shore he forgot to anchor it properly, only now with his future stretched out before him can he see what he should have seen all along that the letters CA and LA are missing from – have fallen off – the stamp. It should read – that's right – COCA COLA. His predecessor had stamped on regardless and he will too. The story's a joke right? Best forgotten. A naïve allegory about the role of the writer in late capitalist modes of production. One-dimensional claptrap. Right?

CHRIS just smiles.

LEO crushes his empty beer can and chucks it.

I always regretted letting it be published in the university magazine. I was too desperate. But I'd give anything to possess the spontaneity that wrote that story again. To taste that again. To have no reputation. No name. To feel the future in front of me like a bright meadow or an open sea. Like you –

He kisses CHRIS.

They kiss.

It's okay. No one's watching.

They kiss.

*

CHRIS, OLIVER.

CHRIS is reading a book.

OLIVER practising his trombone. Bach.

CHRIS   *(Laughing.)* This is good. This is really good stuff.

Ha!

OLIVER hits a wrong note.

Starts phrase again.

*

CHRIS, LYDIA, OLIVIA.

CHRIS and LYDIA watch OLIVIA sleeping.

LYDIA   *(Softly.)* Isn't she beautiful.

CHRIS	Let's go. Lydia please.
LYDIA	Don't worry she's a heavy sleeper, always has been.
CHRIS	We shouldn't be here. What if she wakes up? What if someone comes in?
LYDIA	Chris, relax. She's not going to wake up. Everyone's asleep. Besides if they come in we're checking out a noise. That you saw a strange light moving –
CHRIS	I don't want us to be here. My job.
LYDIA	I wonder what she's dreaming. She looks so peaceful.

Slight pause.

They used to speak their own language – the twins – their own secret language. Leo and I never understood. It faded with time. They hardly use it now. Leo put it in a play once. All that jabbering.

Pause.

She wants to be a surgeon. She's always been fascinated by the insides of things. She'll be a good surgeon.

Pause.

Listen to her breathe

Silence.

| CHRIS | Lydia, why are we here? |
| LYDIA | No special reason. I've always done this on nights when I can't sleep, watched them sleeping instead. First, in the room they shared. Then, in their own rooms. They're growing apart. They grow so fast. And the |

trees around the house grow. Only I stay the same.

Brushes OLIVIA's hair behind her ear. Strokes her cheek.

OLIVIA   *(Still asleep.)* Chris.

LYDIA   Did she say your name?

Pause.

LYDIA strokes OLIVIA's cheek, brushes her fingers across OLIVIA's lips.

OLIVIA   *(Still asleep.)* Chris.

Beat.

LYDIA   Thought so.

*

CHRIS, OLIVIA, OLIVER, LEO, LYDIA.

Eating a meal together.

CHRIS   It's really good. Wow.

LEO   They were at it all day.

LYDIA   You've made quite an impression Chris. They never cook like this for us.

OLIVIA   That's tea-smoked duck with juniper berries and cassia bark. Oliver did the beans.

OLIVER   And the nettle soup!

OLIVIA   That's black cloud ear. It's a fungus.

CHRIS   Thanks. Both of you. It's just great. I'm spoilt. *(Laughs.)* Will I get this treatment after every rostered day off?

OLIVIA   It's our welcome back treat. We imagined you eating all by yourself at home. Probably some food from the supermarket that came in polystyrene and had to be heated up in a microwave. We pictured you eating in front of the television, watching sport or something. It was too brutal.

CHRIS   *(Laughing.)* I don't have a microwave.

OLIVER   You should see the guy who replaces you on your days off. He's a horror.

OLIVIA   Ohmygod – a beast.

LEO   The kids call him 'The Anti-Chris'.

OLIVER   He just stands out there looking dumb. But you can tell he thinks he's like really tough and important. He's got a Rambo complex.

OLIVIA   And he's a perv.

OLIVER   Olivia caught him staring into her bedroom window. He's probably like an ex-con. Have you seen his tats? The panther?

LYDIA   Oliver. That's enough.

         (To CHRIS.) More wine?

CHRIS   Yeah. Thanks.

         A window smashes.

         Everyone screams except CHRIS.

         Stay here. Keep calm. Don't go outside. I'm on it.

*

CHRIS, LYDIA, LEO.

Silence.

CHRIS   You should sleep. Nothing more you can do
               tonight. They won't come back.

               Silence.

               Go to bed. The glass will be replaced
               tomorrow and we'll install extra cameras
               around the fence. The garden too. We'll be
               watching.

               Pause.

               They're only trying to scare you. They want
               you scared. You're safe. I'm here. Go to
               sleep.

               Silence.

                              *

CHRIS.

Watches.

Long silence.

Radio static.

                              *

CHRIS, OLIVER.

OLIVER   It's not going very well, is it. I don't feel
               exactly like safe.

CHRIS   Go to bed Oliver. It's late.

OLIVER	There's a hole in the house where a window should be. How am I supposed to sleep?
CHRIS	It'll get fixed tomorrow.
OLIVER	Fixed?
CHRIS	Replaced.
	Pause.
	Go to bed.
OLIVER	I'm gonna stay out here with you. Keep watch. Make sure nothing happens.
	Silence

*

CHRIS, LYDIA.

LYDIA	I hardly ever see you.
CHRIS	I'm here everyday except Monday.
LYDIA	You know what I mean. Alone.
	Beat.
	We've got an hour.

*

CHRIS, LEO.

LEO	May I see your gun?
CHRIS	No Leo sorry I can't.
LEO	C'mon Chris. I just want to have a look.
CHRIS	It's against regulations.

LEO	What do we care about regulations?
	He kisses CHRIS. Slight pause.
	Chris, I pay large sums of money to the people who employ you to come and stand out here under the stars six nights a week. The gun's to protect me and my family.
	Slight pause.
	I want to feel the weight – how it fits in my hand – your gun.
	Beat.
	When I write about you Chris, I want my facts right.
	Pause.
CHRIS	This is really against all regulations.
	Hands the gun to LEO.
LEO	It's light, lighter than it looks. I've made people hold them in my stories – once even in a play – but can you believe it never held one myself. Thought it'd be heavier. Know what Chekhov said about guns? Course you don't. Never put a loaded weapon on stage if no-one is thinking about firing it.
	He stands with his arms by his sides. The gun in one hand.
	He stands like that for a long time. Just staring into the shadows.
	Very long silence.
CHRIS	Hey.
	Silence.

Leo.

Hey Leo.

Leo.

Leo, better give it back now.

Pause.

LEO turns and points the gun at CHRIS.

Silence.

LEO   Save me Chris.

*

CHRIS, OLIVIA.

Making out.

CHRIS   I want to take you for a drive.

OLIVIA   What?

CHRIS   Take you driving. I –

OLIVIA   *(Laughs.)* Now?

CHRIS   When I have a day off I want you to come for a drive with me.

OLIVIA   In a car?

CHRIS   Yes.

OLIVIA   Where?

CHRIS   We'll drive out of the city, follow our noses, get lost, maybe end up at a beach or in the desert or the mountains, walk around a bit, or just keep driving listening to whatever radio stations we pick up. I'd like that.

OLIVIA   Chris this is just for here, okay? I like
                  kissing you. I like all the stuff we do but it's
                  just for here. Okay?

                  Pause.

                  Kiss me.

                  They make out.

                                        *

CHRIS, OLIVER.

CHRIS and OLIVER are playing a video game. CHRIS is really concentrating.

OLIVER   Okay. Follow me. Down the stairs. Yep.
                  Okay. No not there. Get out of the hall.
                  There's snipers. Yep. In there. No not that
                  one. That door doesn't open. Yep. Yep.
                  Keep coming. You stuck or what? You're
                  going in circles. Man. *(Reaches over and hits
                  a button on CHRIS' controller.)* Okay. Now
                  you're good, just stay close. When we get to
                  the railing, there's gonna be heaps of guys.
                  Take out the ones coming up the ladders
                  first. And shoot the barrels.

CHRIS   What for?

OLIVER   They blow up.

                  Slight pause.

                  Okay. Good. Yep. Yep. Yep. Him. Him.
                  Him. Get him. Nup. You're dead. You have
                  to wait until you rejuvenate.

                  CHRIS stops playing.

                  *OLIVER keeps going, thumbs hitting buttons on the
                  controller.*

Silence. OLIVER playing.

You know you're not the only one don't you. In case you thought you were like the special one. You're not her first and you're not her *only one.*

Pause.

The slut.

CHRIS Don't talk about her like that.

OLIVER *(Still playing.)* About who? Which one? Which one do you like better? Which slut? Which one is the better fuck?

Beat.

You're alive again. Start shooting. Or you'll get killed again. Shoot. Don't just stand there like a dickhead. You don't just stand there. Move. Shoot. You're dead again.

Beat.

Do you think Olivia doesn't tell me everything. Did you think your secret was safe with her? I can hear her thoughts, Chris. I know. I fucking –

CHRIS attacks OLIVER.

They brawl. It's desperate and brutal.

OLIVER gets CHRIS' gun from the holster and forces it into CHRIS's mouth.

Long silence.

CHRIS Oliver.

Oliver.

Put it down.

Put it down. Okay?

Put it down mate.

Oliver, put it down.

Silence. OLIVER, trembling.

Oliver. I –

OLIVER removes the gun from CHRIS' mouth. Kisses CHRIS.

After a few seconds, he drops the gun.

CHRIS holsters the gun.

OLIVER   *(Sobbing.)* I love you.

*

CHRIS.

Guarding.

Cracks knuckles.

Removes gun from holster and aims it into shadows.

A long silence.

CHRIS   Stay back.

*

CHRIS, OLIVIA, OLIVER.

OLIVIA and OLIVER sing 'I Would Die For You' by Prince. Sometimes, OLIVER accompanies on trombone. CHRIS listens.

OLIVIA   Did you like it?

CHRIS   Yes. Thank you. Thank you both.

*

CHRIS, LEO, LYDIA, OLIVIA, OLIVER.

They stare into the pool.

OLIVIA   Who'd do that?

                 Silence.

OLIVER   It's just floating there.

                 Silence.

                 CHRIS fishes the carcass of a dog out of the pool.

*

CHRIS, LYDIA.

LYDIA   Who would do that? The children wanted
a dog so very much when they were little.
They adored it. Played with it all the time.
Incorporated it into their games. Dressed
it up. Took it on endless walks. Eventually
of course, the novelty wore off and the dog
disappeared into the background, became
part of the furniture. It'd sit at our feet and
we'd stroke it's head while we watched TV.
It stared up at us. Desperate to be loved
again. Those eyes. We took turns opening
the cans and feeding it. Well, we *used to*
when we had those family rosters of chores
stuck on the fridge – our names and jobs
in a grid in different coloured textas. Now,
it's whoever remembers — mostly that's
Leo – because he's patient and well the dog
always had a soft spot for him, followed him
around or sat and watched him write like

some fucking moulting muse. I bet we'll be finding its hair around here forever.

CHRIS   You should go inside. It's not safe.

*

CHRIS.

Very alert.

Listening for something in the shadows.

CHRIS   *(Whispering.)* I know you're there. I know you're out there.

Beat.

Don't come any closer.

Don't fucking –

*

CHRIS, LYDIA.

CHRIS asleep.

LYDIA   Chris.

Chris.

Hey Chris.

She tries to wake CHRIS.

Chris. Wake up.

She shakes CHRIS.

Wake –

She stares into the night.

*

CHRIS, OLIVIA, OLIVER.

The twins are dressed identically.

They speak in their secret language.

They seem to be discussing Chris.

CHRIS   STOP. PLEASE.

                       They continue, louder.

                       IT'S ME. CHRIS.

                       STOP JABBERING.

                       They won't stop.

                       Louder.

*

CHRIS.

Just stares into the shadows.

Tries to light a smoke. The lighter jams. Eventually gets it lit. Smokes.

Trembles and trembles.

*

CHRIS, LEO, LYDIA.

LEO and LYDIA are making love.

LYDIA   Quiet.

                       Leo.

                       Keep it down.

You'll wake the children.

CHRIS watches.

*

CHRIS, OLIVER.

CHRIS cleans the gun.

OLIVER   I miss you when you're not here. It's hell. I wait for you to come. All I think about is you. Let's go away from here. Let's start again.

He holds CHRIS. Kisses CHRIS' neck.

*

CHRIS, OLIVIA.

Asleep together, embracing.

CHRIS wakes suddenly from a bad dream. Distressed.

OLIVIA   *(Woken by CHRIS.)* It's okay, sweetheart, it's okay.

CHRIS   I dreamed they found me. I dreamed they were showing me. I was on display.

OLIVIA   It's okay. You're with me. You're safe.

*

CHRIS, LYDIA.

CHRIS fucking LYDIA.

He is distressed.

LYDIA   *(Gently.)* It's okay.

              It's okay.

Chris darling, it's okay.

You're safe.

*

CHRIS, LEO.

LEO fucking CHRIS.

CHRIS   Quieter.

Leo.

Keep it down a bit.

You'll wake the others.

*

CHRIS, OLIVER.

They hold each other.

CHRIS   Beautiful night. So clear. All the stars.

Silence.

I love you.

OLIVER   I love you.

Silence.

*

OLIVIA, OLIVER, LEO, LYDIA, CHRIS.

They eat dinner in silence.

CHRIS   *(To OLIVIA.)* Can you pass me the… um vinaigrette?

She does.

Long silence.

*

CHRIS.

Very long silence.

CHRIS stands watch.

Hears a noise in the shadows,

A gunshot.

CHRIS collapses.

Lies bleeding.

*

Empty stage. Nothing.

Light shifting.

*

LEO   I dreamed that we all made love. My wife, my children, Chris, and I. The lights were low. As if a single candle flickered on the walls of our cave. Our love-making was tender. Without shame. Like they say Eden was. In the dream, we take time to make each other feel good. We feel very good. Full of love. Without lack.

             Silence.

I do not have the words to accurately
describe what happened in my family. I am
supposed to have the capacity to render the
hidden side of being in words. To say what
is unsaid. That's my talent – it's what's been
expected of me since I was young and it's
what I am celebrated for – but if you ask me
to describe Chris standing by the pool in
his uniform I cannot. Will not. I fail. Before
he came to us, my writing had become a
factory. Now he's gone, I'll send the workers
home. I'll unplug the great machines, shred
the files in the filing cabinets. I'll open the
gates so anyone can come in and take what
they want. Let them empty the halls. I'm
walking away. There'll be no more plays, no
more poems, no more stories. No father. No
husband. No writer. I won't go on without
him. I will silence the voices in my head
and erase the words before they hit the
page. No more words.

*

OLIVER.

Stands masturbating. Eyes closed. Mouth open. In a kind of trance.

*

LYDIA   On the night of the children's sixteenth
               birthday, I invited Chris inside on a whim.
               I wanted to see what would happen if she
               came inside. If she joined our family. It was
               a sudden impulse, a whim. Now she's gone,
               I think I understand a little how it is to feel

hollow. Losing Chris has hollowed me. I'm scraped out.

Silence.

I no longer feel like a stranger in my house. It's stopped exploding in slow motion. Leo will leave soon and the children are hardly there but I want to stay. I like floating on my back in the pool and looking up at the stars. I like being close to the places where Chris and I made love. At night, I look for Chris on the other side of the glass. I want her to come home. I'm waiting.

*

LEO.

Stands masturbating. Eyes closed. Mouth open. Desperate.

*

OLIVIA   I never wanted to write like Dad. It wasn't my dream. It was Oliver's. That was a basic difference between us. When we shared a room, he'd stay awake long after we were supposed to be asleep, reading under his sheets by torchlight or scratching away in a notebook. When he wasn't around, I read his diary – his tiny, obsessive scrawls like ant trails – and recognised myself in his experiments. His first poems. I was his incandescent double, his female self, the angel at the annunciation, death's bride riding a pale horse, veil trailing behind. It scared me – watching him change, becoming less me, less us, more

dad. My reality was not split like his. I
believed in sensations, pleasure – the body
– and I sought pleasures out in the usual
things. Sport – cross country running
for example – swimming, dancing, food,
drugs, sex. I discovered sex early and was
never ashamed. When Chris came along,
I thought he was a godsend. Out there,
every night, for my pleasure. I lay in bed
at night and watched him on the other
side of the glass standing out there in the
moonlight. I wet my fingers and touched
myself. Imagined him looking in, watching
me. It surprised me after Chris left when
I began to write things down. I didn't sit
down like planning to write, it just sort of
came out. Now I ask myself if I was really
preparing for this all along – while Oliver
sat hunched at his computer composing his
plays and poems, while I pored over Da
Vinci's drawings of the body or Vesalius'
De humani corpis fabrica or online videos of
vivisections – was I really preparing myself
for this moment when writing would begin?
I have discovered that I can split myself
in two. Make myself male and female. I
will invent a character named Chris who
is male and female. And Chris will stand
in the moonlight on the other side of the
glass. Chris will watch us and we will watch
Chris. I will invent a mother named Lydia
and send her to ask if Chris is lonely. She
will invite Chris inside and join us. Like a
mother should.

*

LYDIA.

Masturbates. Weeps. Still masturbating.

*

OLIVER   I'd watched Chris for a long time before we sat next to each other at my birthday – our birthday. I watched her at night patrolling the garden or standing by the pool. The reflections of the pool rippling on her uniform. She looked like a statue. I already had a crush on her, but I'd never spoken to her. I hadn't even imagined it was possible, you know, talking to Chris, approaching Chris, like walking up to her and striking up a conversation. She was unapproachable. So I was pretty nervous when she was suddenly sitting there between me and Olivia at our birthday dinner. I hardly spoke and when I did the words stuck in my mouth or came out wrong. I remember that my ass was kinda tender. Nothing bad. Just tender like I could feel it while I sat there because taking a shower before getting dressed for dinner, I'd slipped a finger in my ass while I jerked off, thinking of Chris, imagining that Chris had left her post and used her keys to let herself into the bathroom, that it was her hand not mine on my cock, her finger not mine pressing into my ass when I came against the tiles. I told Chris about this once – when we knew each other and I felt safe with her – and she laughed about my shyness saying she'd been the shy one. She told me that I had looked beautiful all dressed up for my birthday. That she'd noticed that. She was the first person who saw me as me, not as a version of my sister or my father. That meant something. I didn't tell the detectives anything. I didn't betray her secret. I tried to find her. Went to her firm. Searched all over town. Why won't anyone tell me where she is? She's in trouble, she needs my protection. There are signs everywhere warning me that she is in danger. Walking home yesterday, I saw a pigeon eating vomit by the road. I saw a cloud that looked like a slaughtered dog. I read that a lion escaped from the zoo and is loose in the city. These are signs that Chris needs me. There are signs everywhere. I love her. I need to get away. I need to find Chris.

*

OLIVIA.

Lies on her belly, masturbating. She sucks her fingers, touches between her legs.

Looks out into the night.

OLIVIA   Chris. Chris. Chris. Chris. Chris. Chris.
Chris. Chris. Chris. Chris. Chris. Chris.
Chris. Chris. Chris. Chris. Chris. Chris.
Chris. Chris. Chris. Chris. Chris. Chris.
Chris. Chris. Chris. Chris. Chris. Chris.
Chris. Chris. Chris. Chris. Chris. Chris.
Chris. Chris. Chris. Chris. Chris. Chris.
Chris. Chris. Chris. Chris. Chris. Chris.
Chris. Chris. Chris. Chris. Chris. Chris.
Chris. Chris. Chris. Chris. Chris. Chris.
Chris. Chris. Chris. Chris. Chris. *(Her orgasm.)* Chris. Chris. Chris. Chris. Chris.

Chris. *(Sobbing.)* Chris. Chris. Chris. Chris.
Chris. Chris. Chris. Chris. Chris. Chris.

*

CHRIS.

Dressed as security guard. A slightly different uniform.

CHRIS   I have a recurring nightmare where I am
                 on display in a circus or museum. I'm on a
                 stage with curtains and coloured lights. Or
                 behind glass. I have to stand there naked
                 for a really long time and it hurts. I think
                 I'm going to collapse. My legs shake. And
                 all these people are staring at me. They just
                 stare and stare.

                 Pause.

                 Leo told me the story of Hermaphroditus.
                 He pointed out the Pleiades in the night
                 sky. He told me that the mother of Hermes,
                 Maia, was one of those stars. Hermes
                 was the god of astronomy, god of herds
                 and trade and language and thievery and
                 omens. The Romans called him Mercury.
                 Like the planet. He was also protector
                 of the home. Like me. *(Laughs.)* Hermes
                 loved Aphrodite. She was the goddess
                 of love and beauty and sexuality, Venus
                 to the Romans. Like the bright star I
                 watched rise over the pool on clear nights.
                 She gave birth to a child – a two sexed
                 child – Hermaphroditus. Leo said that
                 Hermaphroditus is a god who appears at
                 certain times among humans. With a body
                 which is beautiful and delicate like that of
                 a woman but has the masculine quality and

vigour of a man. Leo said Hermaphroditus is irresistible.

I don't know.

After the accident, it was touch and go. The doctors told me I was at death's door. When I finally woke, I was in a pale room in a hospital and the sun was streaming through a window. Everyone was very kind to me. I told them about my dreams of vegetation. The smell of decaying plants, vines. After they'd conducted tests and interviews and written reports, I was declared fit to work again. The firm agreed to a transfer – they have branches everywhere – and I began again here. I'm here six nights of the week. There are eighteen floors and even though they're all empty, I've got plenty to do. I check my monitors or patrol the floors. I prefer being alone. It's why I chose the job in the first place. Sometimes, I'll stand at one of the huge windows and just stare out at the city. The lights. It makes me feel calm. I feel safer here. There's not so many you know *dramas* here. But I stay alert. You've got to.

*

OLIVIA, OLIVER, LEO, LYDIA.

The family sit at the dinner table eating artichokes and sipping champagne. They are dressed for a special occasion. They tear leaves from the artichokes and dip the flesh in melted butter or vinaigrette.

LYDIA   *(To OLIVER.)* Can you please pass me the vinaigrette?

He does.

Thank you darling.

*

CHRIS.

CHRIS removes uniform.

Stands naked.

Just breathes and breathes.

Lights fade.

THE STARS

Characters

MIKE, late 30s

A GIRL, 17 or 18

A long table. Food. Alcohol.

An incredibly fat man, MIKE, sits there, stuffing his face.

A GIRL, 17 or 18, but could look younger, at the other end of the table. She just sits there, watching MIKE. She keeps her eyes on him for the duration of his performance. Barely reacts. Minimal, natural movement. Maybe she has a bottle of water and a glass from which she takes an occasional drink.

MIKE   *(Speaking with mouth full.)* She looks down at me. I look up at her, over her naked belly. She stares. Wide-eyed. With pleasure or discomfort? Pleasure, of course. Her belly is tense, her spread legs quiver, and her wide eyes stare up at me. Hold on – if it's pleasure shouldn't they be shut? Shouldn't her neck be reclining and her mouth be ever so slightly open? And why isn't she moaning?

He drinks wine. Eats.

She looks like a stunned animal. Like a deer on a mountain road. A deer who wandered from the forest onto a moonlit mountain road. She stares up at me like that deer staring into the eyes of a motorist rounding the bend of a mountain road. Like I'm the driver out for a midnight drive suddenly coming across this stunned deer in the middle of the road. Like I'm driving my drop-top convertible up the mountain road at midnight, wind in my hair, tearing around hairpin bends, when too late I see this deer frozen in the moonlight, swerve to avoid, lose control, crash through the barrier, soar off the cliff, spin seemingly in slow motion above the moonlit pines before plummeting to fiery death. The deer, hearing the explosion in the valley below, springs from the road into the depths of the forest.

Eats. Drinks.

Unless of course the deer wasn't startled by a convertible rounding the corner but by a truck loaded with felled pines driven by a trucker who, knowing the mountain roads like the back of his hairy hand, is driving on auto-pilot, some pop song from childhood bouncing around his head, as he rounds the corner and, confronted with the stunned deer in his headlights, hits the brakes too hard for a truck loaded with felled pines travelling at reckless speed around a hairpin bend which now jack-knifes and skids, collecting the moonlit deer which was *just standing there* like a fucking statue of a deer, and is killed upon impact, dragged under the truck's six locked wheels as it crashes through the safety barrier and soars above the pines, suspended impossibly in the moonlight before it plummets and careens down the embankment splintering pines, cabin jerking and rolling while the white knuckled driver at the wheel, no longer on auto-pilot, hopelessly tries to correct the steering wheel that now has a life of its own, a tremendous crack echoes through the previously still night and a resounding boom startles the animals who live in the forest as the fuel tank explodes, the cabin is engulfed in flames, that pop song from childhood slithers in the driver's burning head like a demonic *ear-worm,* the truck now a fireball tearing through the valley like a comet or an *alien pod* crashing through the pines.

Stops eating.

She looks down at me, I look up at her, my tongue in her cunt. She's like a stunned animal. Why's she staring like that? What's wrong? I know how to pleasure her. I know pleasure. I've got my techniques. Ask anyone.

He closes his eyes, sticks his tongue out, makes 'pussy-eating' sounds.

Maybe it really was an alien pod fallen from the stars crashing through the forest which the driver of the white drop-top sports-car saw hurtle over him and plough through the valley like a comet and now he's tearing around the mountain bends searching the impact zone for signs of life.

Briefly makes 'pussy-eating' sounds again.

What does he hope to find in the wreckage of the flaming pod? Alien life crash-landed on our planet? Yes. He wants to meet someone out of this world. He wants first contact. With a new species. Someone *totally new*. Someone who might offer him a way out of his lonely, empty life. Someone to shake up a life that, according to him, has become dull, empty and increasingly meaningless. Just now a splendid, angelic creature – who appears to be an astoundingly beautiful female of his species but is actually an alien – climbs out of the wreckage. Her glittering skin is totally different from human girl skin. The flames of the burning pod and the scorched forest shimmer on her skin. Her eyes are not the same as human eyes either. They're two black pools where he sees two miniature versions of himself mirrored, dressed in his shiny white suit by Maison Martin Margiela, walking through the flames towards her. He takes the alien girl in his arms and carries her from the wreckage through the charred forest to his drop-top coupé. This is exactly what he secretly hoped for when he set out from his underground garage and sped aimlessly through the night, tearing around the moonlit bends.

Drinks wine. Stuffs his face.

This is exactly the sort of *miracle* he was secretly hoping for but didn't admit even to himself. And now she's asleep on the calf-skin seat beside him. Asleep or passed out from shock. Her body is covered in tiny scratches but otherwise unharmed. She looks peaceful. Glittering on the calf-skin car seat.

Drinks.

When she wakes on the silk sheets of his king-sized bed, she has no idea where she is or how she got there. Her memory is blank. An erased disk. She closes her eyes. Sees only stars. A shower of stars in the void. The loss of her memory doesn't make her panic like you'd think. Well, only for an instant when she first opens her too-wide-alien-eyes and sees the unfamiliar room and the strange man above her does she freak out. Her breath quickens and her eyes dart about like a trapped animal but he holds her down and lets her fight his grip until she's spent. With time, she accepts the room and the man watching her from the end of the bed. No, she doesn't panic like you'd think she would. Not any more. No visible signs of trauma. Gradually, she comes to accept her new surroundings.

Wipes mouth with napkin.

He dresses her. Shows her his mansion. She wanders round barefoot. Stands at the window, hand resting against the glass, staring out at the grounds. Every now and then, a deer wanders across the lawn and meets her eyes. The man is probably sitting at his piano, working. It's as if the music perfectly describes the instant. The alien at the glass. The deer. The late afternoon sun stretching her shadow across the parquetry.

A beatific smile.

By watching television, she learns his language. And if she has secret longings or unspoken urges, she doesn't speak them out loud. She watches him working. Stands at the glass. Copies the television. They eat elaborate meals prepared by staff who live in a separate area of the compound. Staff who are not permitted to enter his quarters, not at least while she's conscious. The staff consider his new rules eccentric but comply because a.) they're used to satisfying his whims, b.) they believe in his genius, c.) they want to keep their well paid jobs. *It's a dog eat dog world out there.* Like I said, they eat elaborate meals together. Just the two of them. Sat at either end of the long dining table. Soft music playing.

Picks at food.

He's happier than he was before he found her. Less lonely. He imagines she understands him. That finally someone understands his loneliness. The loneliness that inspires his music. The loneliness that echoes in the footfalls of her bare feet on the parquetry floor. The loneliness of her breath forming circles of condensation on the glass. That lonely hum of the fuel injected engine of his shiny convertible when he takes her on midnight drives through the mountains or deserted coastal roads. Sometimes when he's absolutely certain no-one's around, he parks by the ocean and they walk on the sand, holding hands in the moonlight. On hot nights, they undress and swim out beyond the breakers. She floats on her back, looks up at the stars and is filled with a terrible ache. She'd like to describe the hollowness she feels inside but she doesn't possess the words. The ache doesn't sound like his music. No, it's a roar. Like the waves. Like the wind in the pines. Like a forest fire. She stands at the glass listening to him play. Her skin doesn't glitter anymore. Her eyes are like everyone else's. The sky is filled with dead planets.

Dabs mouth with napkin.

She looks down at me. I look up at her. Along her belly. She's stares wide-eyed while I lick her pussy the way I know how. Why is she looking at me like that? Like a stunned animal or a victim working up the courage to beg someone to stop doing something. Fuck's sake. I lick the alphabet on her pussy. A to Z. It's a tried and true technique, guaranteed to hit the spot. But nothing. She just stares at the ceiling. She says, *the sky is filled with dead planets, help me, somebody help me please.* It's pathetic.

Silence. Stares at his food.

She wanders the corridors while he sits there staring at his food. She can't stand her life. *Help me. I'm trapped.* She's like an injured doe trailing mud and blood on the pristine carpets. She looks in empty rooms, furniture covered with plastic. Once, he finds her curled up on the floor, staring at whales on the TV. All these bleeding whales in the surf. They're always killing whales. She doesn't even see him. Like she forgot he exists.

Silence. Eating. Drinking.

It wasn't always like this. He wasn't always a recluse. He didn't always live in a compound. No. He didn't always have a garage with expensive cars and a walk-in-wardrobe with chic white suits hanging in it. Not when he was a kid on the corner keeping watch in that black puffy jacket designed for Arctic conditions. Hands in pockets, breath white in the sub-zero air. On the corner with his boys. White clouds floating from their mouths when they laughed or cussed. Hanging out under freeway overpasses, throwing rocks at bottles. Spraying their names in paint on walls and trains. Names like PHASE, RIFF 180, PVOY, REK ONE. Names they wrote in train yards and abandoned housing complexes to get fame. They knew what was going on in each others' heads because they were all going through the same shit. They knew what it was like to come home and find mum passed out on the couch, face

dirty, a half-eaten bowl of cereal on her lap,
empty drug packets on the floor and some
man they'd never met before saying hello
son as he climbed the stairs to their little
brother's bedroom, the little brother they'd
do anything to protect. Who knows about
his life now? Who knows the details of his
life now? *The sky is filled with dead planets.*
She actually says that, tracing her fingers
in the condensation vapours on the glass.
Where'd she learn stuff like that? *The sky's
filled with dead planets. I'm a prisoner here.
Please. I just want to go home.*

Silence. He eats.

Jesus Fucking Christ. Everything tastes the
same. This – *(He takes a mouthful of food.)*
– and this – *(A mouthful of something else.)*
– and this – *(Another mouthful.)* exactly the
fucking same. They bring the food and I eat
it. *(With mouth full.)* Don't even recognise
myself anymore. When did I get so fat?

*He closes his eyes, sticks out his tongue, acts like he's
eating pussy again.*

She said you're trying too hard. Staring
at me like I was some sort of sick animal
feasting between her thighs. *You're trying too
hard. I don't even know you anymore.* And just
got up and walked out. Through the glass
doors, out of my life.

He undresses.

Now I'm all alone. Like an actor sitting
in a dressing room staring at one of those
mirrors surrounded by light bulbs.

Sits there in a pair of old, dirty, yellowing jocks.

I've taken off my everyday clothes. I'm
about to put on my costume and make up.
I'm staring into my face.

Stares into thin air.

Into the white hole of my face.

He stares.

My mind is like a six lane highway at rush-
hour. I'm standing naked in the middle of
the intersection. The traffic whizzes past.
The cars don't hit me. The trucks don't
plough me down and turn me into road-kill.
Somehow they miss me.

Closes eyes for a bit.

My mind empties of the cars that drive
there. I'm walking along a freeway
overpass. It curves in the purple dusk.
I have no idea where I am or where I'm
going.

He clears his throat.

Excuse me.

He drinks water.

Once upon a time, there was a girl who that
very day had left her father's house. She was
walking along a freeway in the gathering
twilight. Away from her daddy's house.
She'd never felt so alone. Isn't it weird that
not one car drove by? Not one car or truck
or bus or motorcycle. Isn't it *weird*? Purple
dusk settled in the valleys, making her think
of spilled ink and enchanted underwater
kingdoms. She walked and walked.
(Whispers.) I can't believe I'm telling you
this.

Giggles.

That first night, she slept where she fell, exhausted by the roadside, or in a field under the arms of an old dark oak, head resting on her backpack as if it was one of the fluffy down-filled pillows she was used to sleeping on at home. In the coldest hour, just before dawn, she shivered and her teeth chattered and she missed her lovely warm bed, but she was happy to be free. Tiny white clouds of breath floated from her mouth.

A little laugh.

In the morning, she was woken by traffic. A steady stream of cars on the six lane freeway. She politely said thanks but no thanks to the first two drivers who stopped to offer her a lift. Both men. She didn't like the look of them one bit. No way. Uh-uh. The third car was driven by a friendly woman. A mum, young kids in the back. The woman didn't ask too many questions and believed her when she said that she was travelling to the nearest big city where the woman also happened to be driving. 'I'm going to stay with my auntie,' said the girl. 'Is it school holidays?' the woman asked, 'cos it's not for my kids.' 'Oh, our school has special holidays. It's a special school,' she said and the woman left it at that. It was good to be believed and to discover that people believed her. That was going to come in handy. That was going to help her survive in a dog eat dog world. Her father always said it was a dog-eat-dog world out there, *a dog deep fry dog, dog sell greasy dog from drive-thru window to dog in jeep world.*

Yes, that was a total bonus – being believed. On their way into the big city, they sang songs about how big and bright the world is. It was nice. She was happy to be away from her father and his house with all the corridors and confusion.

Pours whiskey, drinks.

And so she made her way into the big, bright world. She grew up fast and learned to get what she wanted. She found a new family. Went to school. Did the things that girls do. She rarely thought of her father and he never looked for her. Or if he did he never found her. With time, she forgot the life they once shared. Those memories belonged to someone else. Like scenes from old films. Like the dead deer buried in the yard, or the dead whales rolling in the bloody surf. Like they never happened. All of which goes to show that people are extremely adaptable. We change our lives according to the flux of fortune, the thrust of ideology, and the fluctuations of the market. That's life isn't it? We're free to be whoever we want, right?

His shit eating grin. Whiskey.

She got herself a new face that her family and friends adored. It helped her get what she wanted. People meeting her for the first time remarked on her lovely smile and overall sweetness. They said she was quite a girl – *a winner.* Oh, she had her fans alright. Her friends were happy to be part of her circle. They enjoyed hanging out with her, talking about boys, literature, world events and movies, the latest clothing trends. But guess what? If you met one of her closest friends and encouraged her to say what she really thought then this so-called friend might admit – given the right circumstances, given your absolute confidence – that, well yes, *of course they were jealous*, who wouldn't be, she's charming and funny and pretty much everybody wants to fuck her, well wouldn't you, she *oozes fuckability* but – *swear you'll never ever tell anyone* – there's this thing – *it's hard to put into words* – some *stain*, some *shadow*, this like *total emptiness* inside her, you know what I mean right? You sense it too right?

Whiskey.

Behind her smile, behind her winning looks, lurks something *chilling*, something *dead*. As if that beauty and charm is a *façade* erected over something *hollow*. That's what her closet friends are saying. That's what her new parents, new brothers and new sisters suspect. They lie in bed at night, staring at the ceiling, and fret about her being totally empty inside. But wait – wait a minute – couldn't it be some kind of *love?* Some kind of *love* buried deep inside her. My God, is that what it is? Some *deeply buried love* they'll never get near, never ever understand?

He begins to laugh. A light, giggly laughter.

Sorry.

He covers his mouth while he giggles.

Why am I even telling you all this?

Tries to gain control of his giggles.

With time – *(Giggles.)* Wait – *(Composes self.)*
With time she leaves girlhood behind. She
leaves the thrills and spills of adolescence
behind and – *(Clears throat.)* – becomes a
woman.

Eats something sweet and creamy.

She develops interests. Does some
modelling. Studies architecture. She's
always accidentally cutting her fingers
while making white card maquettes of
shopping malls and harbour-side concert
halls. She studies cinema theory. *Visual
pleasure and narrative cinema.* And even
though she's initially curious about these
things, she never finds a way to turn that
initial curiosity into something lasting that
might sustain her. She travels a lot. With the
modelling. Later, simply because she enjoys
travelling. She has multiple lovers in various
countries. She likes to – these are her words
– *sample the local cuisine.* Most of her love
affairs are little more than flings but some
become substantial, even last a few years.
Several of her lovers – the ones I was able
too speak to – described her as a passionate,
adventurous lover, *dynamite in the sack.* But
when the line of inquiry got beyond the
superficial, they admitted, after first making
excuses – it was late, they'd had too much to
drink, *look how many bottles we went through*
– that fucking her was like fucking a doll,
an extremely well engineered sex doll that
knew all the moves but inside was chips,
wires and dumb machinery. Then beads of
perspiration appeared – and it wasn't just
the drink – on the foreheads of the grown
men and women who'd been her lovers and

they quickly settled the bill and made their way into whatever night we happened to be meeting in. Excuse me.

Drinks water. Gurgles. Spits it out.

Dry mouth. When she eventually settles down and gets married, it's not out of passion or romance. No-one unlocks that secret love buried deep inside her. No. It just happens. Suddenly they're married. A couple. They meet other couples and cook meals for other couples, eat meals cooked by other couples. When the weather's nice, they go on picnics with other couples and throw their empty bottles into the woods. Eventually they have children of their own and their kids play with other couples' kids. Standing at the window, she watches her children play on the lawn. They look like they've been photographed for a home furnishing catalogue. A circle of condensation forms and dissolves against the glass where her breath falls. She feels like at prisoner. How did she *end up here*? She's filled with a terrible ache. She's suffocating. Trapped.

He puts on a pair of sunglasses.

She walks in, sits down opposite him.

Silence.

'Are you okay?'

Silence.

'Are you okay?'

Silence.

'Say something. Please say something. You just sit there. It's like living with a zombie. And take those ridiculous sunglasses off. Take those fucking things off and look at me.'

Silence.

'Why do you never touch me? Is something wrong with me?'

Silence.

'You never kiss me.'

Silence.

'We've forgotten how to kiss. Remember how we used to kiss? We'd be walking along the street and stop suddenly and kiss like nothing else existed. Remember? We'd say we had *fever,* stop whatever we were doing and kiss like there was no tomorrow.'

Silence.

'Do you have any idea what I did today while you sat here?'

Silence

'The cinema was nearly empty. This guy was sitting a few rows in front. I'd felt his eyes on me in the ticket line. Tough. Like one of those those dumb mean dogs they walk around the streets. I went and sat next to him. He stank. Male, animal, sucking sugary drink from a jumbo container. I undid my belt, pulled my jeans below my knees, took his hand and placed it on my cunt. We stared at the screen – a car exploded – he pushed his fingers inside me, stuck his tongue in my ear and whispered obscenities. He knelt on that filthy carpet littered with candy wrappers and popcorn and spread my legs. He feasted between my thighs. His nails dug into me. It hurt. The screen flickered – palm trees, headlights. I'm leaving.'

Silence.

And she left. Just like that. Walked out. With nothing. Just an overnight bag, make up and a few clothes. She shut the door on her old life, her husband, her *children*. Off to a new city to start a new life. On the plane, something weird happens, a kind of panic attack. She's convinced that the plane will be taken over by terrorists and flown into some target. She watches the other passengers – the men sitting near her or walking up and down the aisles – and is absolutely convinced that a group of them share a secret about a deadly plot to storm the cockpit, take control of the plane and transform it into a suicide weapon. She interprets their behaviour as evidence of the conspiracy. Isn't their behaviour weird? That guy there erasing photos on his phone. And *those guys*, aren't they secretly communicating with each other across the cabin with coded nods and winks and shrugs? Don't they look kind of guilty? Like they have explosives strapped to their chests. Fuck why are they praying all the time. Bent forward in their seats fucking well *praying*. Isn't it *weird*? She's paralysed by fear, sick with it. She huddles – wrapped in her lightweight complimentary blanket – against the curved plastic wall of the cabin. Shaking. Should she talk to the cabin crew or what? She's embarrassed and terrified at the same time. Embarrassed by how *stupid* and *irrational* she's being. Terrified by what she imagines is the *imminent take over* of the plane. Poor little thing. Sick, helpless, stunned animal. Like a victim working up the courage to beg someone to stop doing something. Shivering under the blanket, suppressing sobs. Poor thing.

Silence.

She writes letters to the people she loves even though she knows the recipients will never ever receive them unless *by some miracle* the letters survive the wreckage. She writes to the father she forgot and buried inside her. She writes to her ex-husband, to the children she left behind. She describes the kind of big, bright world she wants the children to grow up in and so the children will know what mummy experienced in the hour before the men took control of the plane and flew it into the target, she draws *death,* an actual picture of *death.*

He closes his eyes for a bit.

The captain requests all passengers to please fasten their seat belts in preparation for landing. She folds away her tray table and stares out the porthole at the clouds piled up like castles. Like oversized animals. Like nebula seen through a super-high-powered telescope. Like slow motion explosions. Everything turns white. They're inside a cloud and everything's white like a city filled with fog or a nightclub dance floor – what do you call that stuff, disco smoke – like a city filled with fog or a nightclub

dance floor completely filled with disco
smoke, like a blank, endlessly rearranging
canvas. Look, the lights on the plane's
wing are blinking in the cloud. Red white
red white in the cloud. In the bright white
nothing. Red white red. The plane jolts
and jerks. She holds on. White knuckled.
Shut your eyes, hold on. Try not to think of
death. Try not to imagine the pilot losing
control. Or the cockpit being stormed. Or
engine failure. Don't think of death as the
blank white world out there. Those slow-
mo explosions. That endless white. That
foggy city. That smoky disco. That vast
canvas. The blinking lights. Is that what
death looks like? The cabin shakes like it's
breaking apart. No one speaks. No one
screams. The passengers don't chatter or
sing hymns. Some have closed eyes. Are
they praying? Or sleeping? Just trying to
stay calm? Strapped in the rattling cabin.
*Will anyone remember me? Who will remember
me?* The wheels of the plane screech as
they touchdown leaving black rubber trails
on the tarmac. The machine slows and is
steered toward the terminal. A hostess asks
everyone to please remain seated until the
fasten seatbelt sign is switched off, thanks
the passengers for choosing to fly with the
airline and wishes them a pleasant onward
journey. The air crew farewell her as she
leaves the plane. The plane whose engines
are cooling now. The plane which will
shortly be re-fuelled and loaded with fresh
in-flight meals, beverages and duty free
goods. She crosses the air-bridge into the
terminal. Past the light-boxes advertising
alcohol, makeup, and bank-loans. She's

totally blank. A giant empty space inside.
Like the inside of a cloud. A nebula.
Jesus, those vibrations. She walks into the
terminal. Towards her new life.

*He removes his underwear. He pushes his cock between
his legs and stands in imitation of a woman.*

She's stands there naked. Her whole life
ahead of her. It's the moment of decision.
Naked in front of the men on the leather
couches. Those men offering her a future.
*Tell me what you need. I'll be whoever you want
me to be.* She says.

Silence.

That look on her face when she's giving the
men they want, what exactly is that look?
Eyes shut, neck back, mouth ever so slightly
open, body quivering. Is that pleasure? Or
is she feigning pleasure?

Sits, naked.

This is it. Her one shot. Her chance to be a
star.

*Takes a plastic bottle of pills, unscrews the lid. Empties
a pile of pills onto the table.*

Hear the wind? Out there. In the desert.

Silence. There is no wind.

I'm sitting in my silver Airstream trailer
between scenes staring at myself in the
mirror. In my white terry towelling robe.
I'm ready for you now.

*Now he adopts two separate voices and attitudes:
the actress in her trailer and her acting teacher, an
older woman.*

'So, what do you want to work on today?'

I don't know. I'm not feeling great.

'I can come back another –'

No. I don't want to be alone.

'It's up to you. You're paying. How's the shoot? They looking after you? I saw John, sweetie, and he's real worried. Says he's never seen you like this. Johnny's worried, sweetie.'

I'm fine.

'He says you're not showing up on time – some days you don't even show up at all. Honey?'

I'm sick of waiting. Nothing to do but stare in the mirror or read magazines. They're never on time. They never shoot what they say they're going to shoot. I'm sick of this trailer, the desert, the wind. I'm a prisoner. Let's go over the scene.

Swallows pills.

'You shouldn't drink so much. And the pills.'

It's fine.

'I'm worried about you sweetie.'

I said I'm fine. Do the scene with me.

'Ready? *(Running lines.)* Do you mind if I sit here?'

Don't see why not.

'I can't work you out, sugar. Who do you belong to?'

No-one.

'Round here they chew women up and spit 'em right out.'

Sorry.

(Prompting.) 'Not me.'

Not me.

'I saw you looking at me before.'

When?

'From the stage, during your act.'

You're mistaken. The lights were blinding. Shit. That's wrong isn't it.

(Prompting.) 'The lights in my eyes.'

You're mistaken. The lights in my eyes blinded me. I never saw you.

'I felt it. We both felt it.'

No.

'There needs to be a kind of creeping panic under this. She wants him and that scares her. She knows he could destroy her. That's what she finds so attractive and terrifying at the same time. Let's go on. So you weren't looking at me?'

I said I wasn't already, didn't I?

'You've got stars in your eyes.'

I think you should leave.

'I don't believe you, sweetie. It's hollow. There's nothing. No inner life. Again. *You've got stars in your eyes.*'

(More intensity.) I think you should leave.

'When we first met. When you first came
to me, you said you wanted to be truthful.
Remember? You said you wanted to grow up
and develop and play serious parts.'

Dramatic.

'The serious dramatic parts. Remember?'

I remember. *I think you should leave.*

'You're drinking too much. And the pills.
You're damaging yourself and your talent.
You've got something precious buried deep
inside you. You can't keep that locked away
forever, sweetie.'

Leave me alone.

'Like some trapped animal.'

(Quietly.) Please leave me alone.

More pills.

'All wide-eyed.'

Please stop.

'Like some kind of victim.'

I want to go home. I'm a prisoner here.
Please –

'Stop whimpering, honey – no one buys
it – and listen. You sit here in your trailer
thinking you're what? The phosphorescent
fucking diamond shining in the centre of
the universe? Well I've got news, sweetie. It
doesn't work like that. You're the property
of the people who bought you. People who
worked hard to make you you. Who took a
risk because they believed in you. And you

what? You piss it away. Ungrateful little cunt.
I thought you wanted this. Don't you want to
be a huge star?'

He nods, head bowed, slowly.

'Every fibre of your fucking being – your
feelings, memories, everything you've ever
thought and done – is your raw material and
you're obliged to use every last scrap of it.
So stop hiding. Stop being fake. And please
show me what you're made of.'

I left everyone who ever loved me. My
father. My husband. My –

'I don't believe you. '

I'm scared.

'Liar.'

I'm involved in some bad, bad shit.

'I need the real you, sweetie.'

Please help me.

'You're trying too hard.'

Help me.

'More.'

I'm suffocating. Please –

Finishes the pills.

Leave me alone.

Speaks in his own voice again from here.

I walked out. The set was deserted. Where
did everyone go? Did they all just *leave*?
The equipment was standing around in the
desert. Big 5k lights on stands, heads bowed

like praying men. Cameras on dolly tracks.
Boom mics on long retractable arms. All
those machines. Like weird animals at rest.
But not a single soul. No cast or crew. No
one. The director's chair stood empty on the
dirt.

He stands slowly. Unsteady on his feet.

The sun lowered behind the jagged
mountains. As if on wires. *Magic hour.* It
glittered and shone on the salt flats. Like the
skin of an alien creature. The shadows of the
machines grew longer and stranger.

*Sways a little, holds table to stay upright. Eyes rolling
in head. Speech slurred.*

The light turned pink to blue. Like ink
spilled over the world. I walked away from
the silver trailer. Away from the abandoned
film set. Out across the desert. I kicked off
my shoes – useless things – and walked
barefoot now. I could feel the warmth of
the day through the soles of my feet. It was
lovely.

The girl stands up.

It was getting dark when I came across
a clump of pre-fab houses. A settlement.
Televisions flickered inside rooms. Women
stood at sinks. Washing dishes. Preparing
dinner. Some kids were drawing with
coloured chalk. Animals and flowers and
rocket ships. On concrete pavers in the
fading light. Staying outside until mum
called them in for dinner or homework or
whatever. Did they even go to school? These
ragtag kids with grot on their faces. I watched
their chalky rainbow hands. Watched them

drawing and playing. And imagined they were mine. That they belonged to me. I thought about the children I'll never have. My insides aren't wired right.

Laughs softly to himself.

A boy saw me standing on the dunes. In the light of the newly risen moon. Watching them. He was absolutely still. Like he'd seen a ghost. Looked right through me. I was like some kind of stunned animal. Caught in the headlights. Standing there. Then slowly, as if in a trance, he raised his arm and pointed at me.

The girl slowly raises her arm and points at him.

The other kids saw me and recognised me. A girl called for her mother. And it was over. I ran. Barefoot in the moonlight. Across the dunes. I didn't want them to catch me. Didn't want to get caught, all come crashing down. I climbed the ridge and when I reached the crest, I saw the ocean. The deserted beach. The moon was a silver ribbon on the water. I undressed. Swam out. Beyond the breakers. Along the silver ribbon.

He bows his head, speaks very softly.

I'm sorry darling girl. I should never have brought you here. Kept you here. I had no right.

His voice choked with emotion, he can barely speak.

You're free.

The girl walks away from the table.

Watches MIKE climb woozily onto the table.

He lies on his back, staring at the ceiling.

Great, silent tears streak his face.

After a while, the girl leaves.

I'm a long way from shore.

I'm floating.

On silver.

The night is huge.

The stars.

Jesus, the stars.

He doesn't move a muscle – is he even breathing?

Lights fade.

GERONIMO

Geronimo was first published in *The White Review*, No. 10, April 2014.

There was a point before folks had left, before we had gotten everybody back on the helicopter and were flying back to base, when they said Geronimo had been killed, and Geronimo was the code name for bin Laden.

President Barack Obama, May 2011

A small group of guys.

Nowhere.

– We're on the ground.

– What?

– Landed. We've –

– We *what?*

– The boys've landed. They're in the compound.

– On the ground.

– Okay. Gotcha.

– Right on.

– What?

– He said, right on.

– Oh yeah right. Right on.

– Is he?

– Shh. Nothing, it's nothing.

– Right on right on.

– Are you sure he's – because I'm –

– It's fine. He's fine.

– Right on baby.

– He's just –

– What?

– Excited.

– Are you sure this is –

– It's fine – what we – it's fine.

– Watch. Just shut up and watch.

Pause.

– Looks good.

– Looking good.

– Yep, looking gooood.

– It's pretty –

– Yeah pretty much what we.

– Good picture.

– Yeah nice.

– What we –

– I like the colours.

– Yeah nice. The colours.

– Real pretty.

– Sublime.

Pause.

– Okay – watch – Okay – ready?

– Ow.

– Ouch.

– Ouch. That hurt.

– That hurt alright. High five.

– Do you want – does anyone need?

– Nah. I'm fine.

– All good.

Pause.

– Right on.

– Right on.

– Yeah, right on.

Pause.

– Don't wanna –

– What?

– Don't wanna, and this is crucial –

– For sure.

– Don't wanna mistake her hysterics for genuine –

– No fucking –

– Emotion.

– Way.

– Hell no.

– Claw.

– What?

– Claw.

– Claw?

– Yeah, like she's clawing.

– On her back – trying to claw.

– The what? The –

– Air. Clawing the air.

– Face.

– Does she think it's a face? Think someone is – what? – on top? On top of her?

– Think she can claw – can claw her way –

– Claw the face off.

– Claw her way the fuck out of there?

– Out of thin air.

– Threat. She's a –

– Weapon, she's got –

– Thin air.

– Ouch.

 Not moving.

– Not so busy moving now.

– Not so busy with *movement* now is she.

– Clawing.

– Flailing.

– Like – like a –

– Not so busy now.

– No.

– Christ.

– Jesus fucking Christ it's down.

– Oh fuck, fuck, fuck.

– Oh fuck, oh Christ.

– We lost one.

– It tilts, hovers and –

– Oh Christ, it can't –

– Fuck fuck fuck.

– Down.

– Hangs. Suspended. Like a –

– Bang.

– Down.

– The blades touch the –

– Concrete.

– And it's over.

– Over and over.

– Torch it.

– Over.

Pause.

– Fine. We'll be fine.

– Us? Of course we'll –

Pause.

The boys? Yeah right the boys. Of course they'll be fine. The boys.

Pause.

– Hey guys.

– What?

– People are worried.

– What?

– Worried, they're worried.

– Worried? About what?

– The name.

– What have people got to worry about?

– The name.

– We're doing this to make them safe –
fucking safe – not worried. For Christ's –

– Worried we got the name wrong.

– It means some things to some people and
might give the wrong you know.

– The name?

– The name yeah. The mission name.

– Fucking people. Which fucking people?

– Well.

– Which fucking people think we got the
name wrong?

– Sensitivities. Cultural –

– Overfuckingsensitivefucking.

– Which people which fucking people?

– Indians. The Indians.

– Native.

– Native – sorry – Americans.

Pause.

– To them it means something, some kind of
hero. Not a villain.

– Definitely not a villain, monster, target.

– Okay. Okay.

– Resistance fighter. Hero.

– Okay.

Pause.

– Sorry?

– Say sorry?

– Sorry say sorry? Who to? What have we got to be sorry about?

– Lawful. Legitimate. Appropriate in every way.

– Okay.

Pause.

– Yes. Right. Okay.

– Nice.

– Nice one, did you see that? Nice one.

– All clear.

Pause.

– I'm like you. Pretty much normal. A normal guy. Like everyone else, I worry my life is going nowhere. You know. Not where it should. Wrong direction. Lost. When I was a kid I thought I'd grow up to do all these you know *amazing* things. Like everyone else. I worry about my weight. What I eat. Chemicals. And the melting. I flew over Greenland once. This chunk of white. Jesus. I felt so small. Strapped in my seat. Helpless. Wow. I like to swim and after I've done my laps I go into the steam-bath. Relax. Just sit there and sweat. Light was coming through the glass bricks. Man. These slats. Shafts. Golden like heaven. Wow. And one of the guys was sitting there, legs crossed, real still. He didn't move for like ages. Fucking forever. Like he was *praying* or something. Finally he leaned over. Bent so I saw his back. And on his back tattooed was Jesus Christ in all his suffering. Nailed. The thorns.

167

And I thought, holy fuck, this is like like *what is this?* Some kinda *training video?* Because I want to believe. I long to believe. And the steam, the golden light, the Suffering Christ. Was this like some kind of *message?* A SIGN? I thought okay I get it. I get this. I could really get into this. I mean I want to believe as much as anyone. The light. His wounds. I'm so lonely. Lonely all the – even with my friends, my *wife.* I'd do anything to belong. To feel that you know bond, belief. Like them. In their deserts. Praying in their huts and air-conditioned compounds. For a better life. To be given, sent, a sign. Some *sign* it's all worthwhile. Hasn't been for nothing. The suffering. Because otherwise what? Oh my fucking. And then what? The body now without spirit. Meat. No longer one of us. Please please not that.

Silence.

– Worn out, exhausted, dead tired, finished, at the end, wasting away.

– Yes.

– But elated.

– What?

– Worn out, exhausted, dead tired, finished but elated.

– At the end, wasting away.

– But elated.

– Yes.

Pause.

– Live.

– What?

– It said, it wants to live.

– What said what?

– It – he – said, live. Please let me live. I want to live.

– Fucking.

– Let me live. Let me live. Please.

Pause.

– Don't do this. Please don't.

– No way.

– No way buddy.

– No way he's becoming a goddam *martyr*.

– Saint.

– Not fucking well one of the *prophets*.

– No way. Not going down like that.

– Don't say –

– Going down – don't say –

– Okay okay. Not parading him. No way.

– Show him? What? Like a show trial?

– No way.

– Trial ha.

– Martyr.

– He's not the victim here.

– Inspire.

– Please. No one needs to actually see him –

– Ha.

– Alive or dead.

– We got him.

– We got the guy.

– Got him we got him.

– Hell yeah.

Silence.

– She came home drunk. I'd been waiting for hours. Fallen asleep somehow. Well not really asleep. I mean how can I sleep when I don't know where she is. Not asleep no. Anyway when I woke up from dozing or whatever, she was just *standing there.* Slurring words. 'Sorry? I've got no reason to say I'm sorry.' She said. 'I don't have to say sorry okay.' Could hardly even talk properly. I must've dozed off again because when I woke the bed was empty. Well, I dragged myself out of bed to go see if she was alright and there she was in her party dress asleep. Upright. Sleeping upright in her party dress. All crumpled dress. Drooling. On the couch. Drool on her party dress. Passed out like that. Laptop open on her lap. Screen asleep. I wanted to know what she'd been looking at. Drunk on the couch looking at what while I slept in the other room? In our bed. What? What was so important? I wanted to know but I didn't wake up the screen and look. I didn't do that. No. I shook her. Shook her and shook her. She just wouldn't wake up. Rag doll in her pretty party dress. Wake up. Saying her name over and over. Shaking her. And when her eyes opened, she looked at me but said nothing. Like I was really

far away. Like down the other end of some
corridor. A shadow down the other end of
some corridor with its blinking light. Pixels.
I got her on her feet. Lifted her up. And she
she she wandered off in like completely the
opposite direction. Away from our room. I
don't know where she thought she was going.
No idea. I've never seen her like that before.
Not like that. Anyway the next day she sat
on the couch, make up all smeared. Her lips
looked like she'd been kissing. Who? And
on TV, they replayed the raid. Dust. She
was in shock. Some kind of *shock*. Like she
didn't know what had happened. How she
got like this. We talked about our way of life.
How we wanted to live. She said she needed
to feel free. She didn't want to feel like she
had to justify herself all the time. It's her
life she can do what she wants. We just had
to you know like *believe* it would work out
and it would. She didn't want other people
telling her how she should live i.e. what was
possible. Or not. She didn't want to be *held
down*. This scene I saw recently. Someone –
was it a film or live footage? A clip of a real
event? Anyway this actor, this guy – it was
out of focus, grainy, blown out – this guy was
holding this other guy down and he –

He demonstrates.

Was repeatedly striking the guy on the
ground. Lifting this brick up and down and
destroying the other guy's head. Up and
down again. This happened. I think it was
real. This white brick in his hand.

Silence.

I wondered how long she would just *sit there* talking about personal freedom.

Silence.

Eventually she crossed the room and knelt at my feet and rested her head on my lap as if this was the only way to make me understand that she was sorry. Because words had failed her now. She needed me to understand that she didn't want to lose me. I held her head in my hands like a glass ball that at any moment I might lift and drop. I held her head and stroked her hair. I told her that she was precious to me. Very precious.

Silence.

– And the body falls.

– Tumbles.

– Weighed and shrouded.

– Into the receiving sea.

– Like?

– Like an old package.

– An aid package.

– Food.

– Sorry?

– Food.

– Like food.

Lights fade.

GLORIA

Gloria will premiere at Griffin Theatre, Sydney, on 3 September, 2016, with the following cast:

GLORIA	Marta Dusseldorp
JARED	Meyne Wyatt
DEREK / MAN	Huw Higginson
MADDIE / THE GIRL	Chloe Baylis
CASSIE / WOMAN	Kristy Best
PAUL	Louis Fontaine / Max Phillips
CLIENT / MAN 2 / KIP / CLIENT	Pierce Wilcox

Directed by Lee Lewis
Associate Director Ben Winspear
Set and costume design by Sophie Fletcher
Lighting design by Luiz Pampolha
A/V design by Toby Knyvett
Sound design by Steve Toulmin
Photographer and Videographer Brett Boardman

Characters

GLORIA, late 40s

JARED, teenager, then 20s

DEREK / MAN, 40 something

MADDIE / THE GIRL, 12

CASSIE / WOMAN, mid-20s

PAUL, 6 or 7

CLIENT / MAN 2 / KIP / MAN / AD, around 30

One.

Living room. Night. A woman sits watching TV. Sound on mute. A small boy beside her. He might be a doll. Or not. Nothing for a while. The woman walks to the kitchen, opens the fridge, stares inside. Finally, she pours a glass of milk which the boy drinks, still watching the television. When he's finished, she rinses the glass and puts it in the dishwasher. She takes a kitchen knife from the drawer and sits beside the boy. He snuggles into her and she strokes his hair. They watch television. The woman cradles the boy. She kisses his head. Stares at the television. A sound like all the air being sucked from a room. TV flickering.

Black.

1.

The apartment.

JARED — At night when I can't sleep, I walk through the rooms. Feet quiet on the carpet. The refrigerator hums. Our house is a stage set and I'm the only living character. The others are puppets. Made of wood, cloth and porcelain. Faces painted on. They lie in their beds attached to strings, snoring, mumbling, farting, until the string jerks and up they get to play their parts. That weird glow. Is it moonlight? Or glare from the city? Don't care anymore. I walk the halls. Open fridge. Drink juice. Pick at leftovers. Not hungry but do it anyway. All that stuff in plastic and foil. Half-eaten. Cold. Balcony. The city lights stop where the sea begins. Points of orange float in the black. Freighters anchored offshore. Out there I'd sleep. On a bunk. In a cabin. Rocked by swell. One day I'll leave and see the world by ship. I'll work hard and when

day is done, the throbbing of the engines
will comfort my sleep. Down in the hull.
Cocooned. I walk through our cold, blue
rooms. I'm the only real character. The
others are puppets. Jerking in their sleep.
Derek dribbles into his pillow. Snores.
Like a tractor dragging machinery. How
can she stand it? Her porcelain face on the
pillow. Kiss her sleeping eyes. They open.
Stare. We're statues. No. We're actors on
the far side of the curtain, listening for the
audience. That hum. We dare not move.
The curtain billows. Her eyes click shut.
She rolls over. On her strings. I walk the
silent rooms. Headphones. Computer. I'm
a sniper taking out targets. Get a position
on the roof, zoom in on a target. I place the
shots where I like. Head or body. Leg if I
want them to fall first. So I don't get bored.
So each kill doesn't feel the same. Or porn.
The clips where the girls talk to the camera
as if the camera is you. I prefer this. When
they're pretending to be with just me, not
some guy or girl or gang-bang. She talks to
me as if I'm in the room with her. In front of
her on the grey carpet. Crawling toward the
sofa where she rips holes in her stockings.
Teasing me about how I can't touch her,
can't *really touch* her. *Bet you wish you could
touch this perfect little pussy.* But she's wrong.
I don't want that. I just want to watch her
contort on the sofa until I fall asleep. I'll
play the game or watch the girl until I'm
asleep. Soon we'll wake, begin the day, play
our parts. The house is quiet. Listen. This is
how our house sounds at night –

Silence.

2.

Living room.

GLORIA	He won't wake up.
DEREK	What?
GLORIA	I called him.
DEREK	Doesn't he have school?
GLORIA	It's a holiday.
DEREK	What for?
GLORIA	I don't know. A study break.
DEREK	So. He's sleeping in. Taking a break.
	He laughs a bit too hard.
GLORIA	I called and called. Went in and shook him but he won't wake up.
DEREK	You shook him?
GLORIA	I said, wake up darling, *uppies tuppies.* And yes gently shook him. But he's out cold. Dribbling into his pillow. Headphones on. Why don't you try?
DEREK	Me?
GLORIA	He shouldn't let the day go to waste.
DEREK	Let him sleep. He's a growing boy.
GLORIA	Sleeping all day won't help him.
DEREK	Gives us time. Alone. We never.
GLORIA	Derek, he's sleeping. In the next.
DEREK	Please baby.
GLORIA	He could wake any. And Maddie.

DEREK	Gloria. Please. We.
GLORIA	Not now.
DEREK	So beautiful.
GLORIA	Another.
DEREK	I want a child.

Pause.

With you.

GLORIA	It's not the right.
DEREK	Of our own.
GLORIA	We've been through this.
DEREK	Our child.

JARED enters.

GLORIA	Breakfast is cold.
JARED	Not hungry. Anyway don't like eggs.
GLORIA	Since when? You always.
JARED	They're slimy.
DEREK	So. Big study day today.
JARED	Big what?
DEREK	Study.
JARED	I'm going out.
GLORIA	Where?
JARED	Out.
GLORIA	Who with?
JARED	You don't know them.
DEREK	What about study?

GLORIA   Leave it, Derek.

JARED   Yeah, Derek. What kind of a name is Derek
                anyway?

DEREK   A name. It's my name.

JARED   Derek. What does that even mean?

DEREK   You really want to know?

JARED   Enlighten me, Derek.

DEREK   It's Old German actually.

JARED   No shit.

DEREK   Theodoric. Ruler of the tribe.

JARED   All hail Theo*dork.*

GLORIA   I watch them. My two beautiful men.

JARED   Who gives someone a name like that? *Derek.*

DEREK   My parents. Did. Obviously.

JARED   You're seriously cracking me up Derek.

GLORIA   My son laughs. Opens the fridge. Picks at
                leftovers. Drinks juice. When he was little,
                just the two of us and I was always working,
                he'd come to rehearsals. Sit in the corner
                and watch. Very quiet. Rapt. Sometimes
                the scene we were rehearsing was too *full
                on* – you know too violent or sex – so he'd
                go off into the green room with one of the
                assistants. I didn't realise – of course it was
                obvious – how much he wanted to watch
                those scenes, especially those scenes. He
                gave the assistant the slip, snuck in. I didn't
                realise. Too *in the moment.* He crouched
                in the shadows. Watched mummy play
                some full on scene. Drenched with gore.
                Butchered. Or having sex. *(Laughs.)* Naked

on the floor going for it you know. All these people watching, taking notes. And him, under a table or behind some scenery – hot little eyes on me – while I feigned pleasure, ecstasy, over and over. What was that like for him? Watching that. What does he remember? God.

Pause.

Whenever I perform these days – which is less and less – he comes to the dress rehearsal and after we talk about what he liked or didn't, what he *got*, what he thought the production – the director – was trying to achieve. He has strong opinions and I like that. Notices things. Details. But he doesn't come to rehearsals anymore. Prefers to do his own thing, hang out with friends.

Pause.

I remember his eyes. In the dark. I play the scene for those eyes.

MADDIE enters. Dressed like a princess.

MADDIE   Hiya.

GLORIA   Hi darling.

Silence. MADDIE goes to DEREK. He runs his fingers through her hair.

Beyond the sliding glass doors, Derek leans on the balcony. His daughter takes his hand. They look to the horizon. Ships in the bay, the blue. He ruffles her hair. I'm alone at the table with my son's plate of untouched eggs. A breeze blows through the open doors. Through our rooms.

3.

Balcony.

MADDIE	Are you're going away again?
DEREK	Just a short trip.
MADDIE	Where to?
DEREK	Singapore.
MADDIE	Can I come?
DEREK	Sweetheart, you're staying here with Gloria. And Jared.
MADDIE	I want to come and eat breakfast with the orangutans.
DEREK	Another time. Promise.
MADDIE	I stand on tippy toes and look down. Everything's tiny.
DEREK	Long way down.
MADDIE	Do you ever feel like jumping?
DEREK	Jumping? Why? I love you and Gloria. And Jared. No way.
MADDIE	Sometimes it pops into my head that I could climb over.
DEREK	Sometimes everyone. High places. Balconies. Just something your brain. Irrational. But we don't do it.
MADDIE	What's irrational?
DEREK	The opposite of rational. You know. What makes us human. How we think. Logic. We don't give into irrational impulses.
MADDIE	Like apes.

DEREK   What? Yes like apes.

MADDIE   Or the orangutans. That's why I want to
                 eat breakfast with them. To experience
                 that. Are the orangutans in Singapore Zoo
                 irrational?

DEREK   They're different from us, sweetheart.
                 Different cognitive architecture.

MADDIE   So thoughts just pop into their heads too?

DEREK   No. Maybe. I don't.

MADDIE   What about Jared? Is he irrational?

DEREK   No. Well. Sometimes, we all can be
                 sweetheart.

MADDIE   I don't want you to jump.

                 Pause.

                 Don't ever jump.

DEREK   I won't.

MADDIE   You'd splatter.

                 They look.

DEREK   Don't think about it.

MADDIE   I'm not.

DEREK   Good.

                 Silence. They watch a plane crossing the sky.

MADDIE   If you love us so much – me, Gloria and
                 Jared – so much you don't want to throw
                 yourself off the balcony and splatter – if
                 that's true – why are you always leaving us?

                 He runs his fingers through her hair.

4.

Bathroom.

Steam from the shower. JARED stands in front of the mirror. He wipes condensation from the glass.

JARED   I'm the only real character. The rest are puppets. I'm crawling toward you. I can hear you. Through the steam. Are you there?

5.

Living room.

Maddie eats breakfast. Derek pretends to be an orangutan. He takes it very seriously, tries to be as natural as possible.

MADDIE   My dad's gone to Singapore. For work. I'm stuck here with his wife and her son. She's not my mummy and he's not my brother. He gives me the total creeps. What about you? Do you ever wish you were back in the jungle? Do you miss your family?

        Pause.

        At least you get to eat really great breakfasts with people from all over the world. That must be fun for you. Or do you just pretend? You're doing a good job. You're convincing.

        He smiles.

        You've got an oversized bite. You should get that corrected. So you don't scare the clients. Like me. You wouldn't want that now would you?

        Pause.

Do thoughts just pop into your head? Dad
said orangutangs have got different cognitive
architecture. Like what? Mini condominiums
with mini people eating miniature breakfasts
in your brain. Or doing something *irrational*
like –

*She makes a crazy face, speaks a phrase or two of
gibberish.*

Like Jared. Walking around the apartment
at night. How's that rational? He stares at
me. Why don't you say something? Do you
miss the jungle? Sad old ape. Do you miss
mummy?

Pause.

More coffee?

She pours him more coffee. He stares at it.

Mummy's dead. I went to her funeral and
threw dirt in her grave. I wore black and
lace. Now we live up here.

Finally, he picks up the cup and takes a sip.

I don't think orangutans actually drink
coffee. I don't think they're *allowed* to drink
coffee.

Beat.

Better go pack, you don't want to miss your
plane.

He finishes his coffee and leaves.

Shithead.

GLORIA clears away the breakfast.

6.

Bathroom.

JARED   I know you're there. I can hear you.
             Through the steam.

7.

Bathroom.

CASSIE showers. Sings to herself. A dreamy pop song.

8.

Living room.

MADDIE practices her routine.

GLORIA   Getting good Maddie, really coming along.

             She watches MADDIE practise.

             What do you call this one? What's this
             routine, sweetheart?

             *MADDIE messes up the routine, trips or tangles her
             ribbons.*

             Sorry, I'm disturbing you.

             MADDIE continues her routine. Twirling.

9.

Bathroom.

CASSIE is drying herself. PAUL watches her.

CASSIE   Mummy needs to get ready, darling. Why
             don't you read a book or play your game.
             Let mummy get ready.

             Pause.

Please darling. Don't make me late.

10.

Living room.

MADDIE is still practicing.

MADDIE — It's just something I made up. From watching clips. You have to keep the ribbons moving. They're not allowed to stop. This is a *twirl* and this is a *spiral* and this is a *snake* and this is *loop the loop*. And look *flowers*. I want to get really good. Compete. I read a comment on one of the blogs and it inspired me, *you've got a dream, protect it, you want something, go get it.* I want to get out there and compete. Do you think daddy will let me? He bought me the ribbons and the ball.

GLORIA — I don't know darling. We haven't discussed it.

MADDIE — But he bought the equipment.

GLORIA — You just need to discuss it with him. When he's back.

MADDIE — I want to see him. Show him my routine.

GLORIA — Soon.

MADDIE stops.

Why did you stop? Not because of me.

MADDIE — It's hard to talk and practice at the same time. Can't concentrate.

GLORIA — He'll be home any day now. I just spoke to him. He's good. Busy.

MADDIE — Did he eat breakfast with the orangutans?

| GLORIA | I don't know sweetheart. He's busy. |

11.

CASSIE's room.

She brushes her hair.

| CASSIE | You okay darling? You're very quiet. Paul? |

12.

Living room.

PAUL plays his video game.

13.

Living room.

DEREK	I'm in this service station all day. It's so boring.
GLORIA	What for?
DEREK	We're running in the new system on the computers. The sales staff have been re-trained and I'm there to keep an eye on things. Make sure there are no glitches. I'm desperate for something to go wrong so I've got something to do. How's Maddie?
GLORIA	Fine. She misses you. She's out on the balcony.
DEREK	On the balcony? Is she okay?
GLORIA	She's fine. Why?
DEREK	No reason.
GLORIA	Don't you trust me with her?

DEREK   I'm just bored. Nothing to do here but read
          magazines.

GLORIA   She's fine. Twirling her ribbon in the breeze.

          Pause.

          We miss you. We all miss you.

14.

CASSIE's room.

CASSIE   I put on my face. Sit at the mirror, paint on
          my eyes and my lips. Colour my cheeks. I'm
          always like this before a date. You know,
          butterflies. What am I in for?

15.

Living room.

GLORIA   In my costume fitting today, Alice the
          costume designer said I had a *banging
          body.* She actually said that. *Babe you've got
          a banging body.* I was trying on this sequin
          dress she wants me to wear in the fourth act.
          This real tight number. She said I was *hot.*
          I'm supposed to look seductive in the fourth
          act. *Really hot.* She was probably trying to
          make me feel better. The play, my body,
          my age. Rehearsals are hard. I worry about
          glitches in my performance.

DEREK   Glitches?

GLORIA   Like repeat a word by accident. Same thing
          twice without realising. Or blanks. Insert
          random blanks.

DEREK   I'm looking for glitches all the time.

GLORIA   I sound fake.

DEREK	All day long.
GLORIA	Do you think I'm fake?
DEREK	I sit behind the counter. A bit to the side. Turning the pages of a magazine. One eye on the transactions. Making sure the programme is running alright. You're not fake.
GLORIA	I'm worried about the kids.
DEREK	I've got my own screen. Plugged into the main system. Where I monitor the transactions.
GLORIA	At rehearsals. I worry about the kids. Alone up here.
DEREK	The programme. Running in. The kids are fine.
GLORIA	What if someone.
DEREK	It's totally safe. They're fine. Beep beep beep. All day long.
GLORIA	Is that why Alice said that about my body because she can see I'm distracted? Not really inside the role. Fuck, is that why Alice said that?
DEREK	There's security. No-one gets in unless they belong. The hallways are monitored. Cameras. The door. It's fine.
GLORIA	You've got a banging body babe. What does that even mean?

DEREK holds her. Kisses her neck.

I miss you. I want you to hold me.

He runs his fingers through her hair.

I miss your touch. Your fingers through my hair.

He strips her or she strips herself. Hard to tell.

Why did she say that?

JARED I'm going out mum.

GLORIA Where?

JARED Out. With friends.

GLORIA Be safe.

JARED Don't worry mum. Don't worry all the time.

JARED leaves.

GLORIA When I was a little girl, there was a river – a secret river – running under the floor. I lived in my cellar. Footsteps on the ceiling. Dragging sounds. Feet, music. Like I was a princess in the turret of a castle and I could hear this faraway music – waltzes, foxtrots, the fandango – carried on the breeze from a magnificent ball where I was supposed to be. There was no ball. There were no windows, no turret. I was in my cellar. Where the walls were cold. Because of the river. Under the floor. Said Daddy. The river was *ancient*. It went right under our house. He saw it every day flowing through the city up there. I'd never been up there, never seen it. He said a real dirty river, polluted and foul. Once he saw a baby carriage floating in it. And another time in the dirty muck there was a rocking horse. Daddy had a solution. How to fix it. Dig a channel. *A whole other river.* Under the dirty river and take away the foul brown river muck. Then the river on top would be crystal clean and

the citizens crossing the bridges or strolling
along the banks wouldn't be disturbed by
the muck any more. Said Daddy. When they
looked down from the bridges or riverbank,
they wouldn't see rubbish and prams and
dead animals – *all sorts of filth* – they'd see a
clear sparkling river. They could even swim
in it again. He said. Jesus. I'm cold. The
breeze. I wish she'd close the door. Close
the door darling. It's windy. Maddie, close
the door. Please sweetheart close the door.
Sweetheart?

16.

Living room.

A knock at the door. CASSIE lets JARED in.

CASSIE	Hi. Welcome.
JARED	Hi.
CASSIE	Thanks for this.
JARED	Hey no problem, happy to help.
CASSIE	He'll watch TV or play his game then sleep. Shouldn't be too late. Bye sweetheart.
PAUL	Bye.
JARED	Have fun.
CASSIE	I'll try. You too. Bye.
JARED	Thanks. Bye.
	CASSIE leaves.
	Paul. Hi. I'm Jared.

17.

Living room.

MADDIE	It's not 'once he saw a baby carriage floating in it.' It's just 'baby.' 'Once he saw a *baby* floating in it and a rocking horse.' The baby carriage – the pram – comes later. 'When they looked down into the river, they wouldn't see rubbish and prams and dead animals.' But the rest was good. You've pretty much got the whole speech down. Wanna do it again?
GLORIA	No thanks darling.
MADDIE	Are there really underground rivers?
GLORIA	I guess so. Under cities. When they build.
MADDIE	But not rivers under rivers. That's just an idea right?
GLORIA	Yes. Fantasy stuff.
MADDIE	So why is her house underground?
GLORIA	Her daddy built it for her.
MADDIE	Because he didn't want her to run away?
GLORIA	Because he wanted to keep her safe.
MADDIE	From what?
GLORIA	Harmful things.
MADDIE	Was she sad?
GLORIA	Sometimes everybody gets sad.
MADDIE	Do you get sad?
GLORIA	When I miss your dad. But he'll be back soon. Shall we watch something fun? The

chefs. Or the dancing. You like that, right?
Ballgowns.

18.

Living room.

JARED   Identical. Same furniture. Same appliances.
               The view. Paul's even playing the same
               game as me. Pretty violent for a kid. He
               switches guns. Assault rifle. Kicks open a
               door. Takes out some guys. Makes his way
               along a grey corridor. In the basement.
               Concrete bunker. Grey corridor. Kicking
               down doors, taking out guys. He's running
               through the compound. Shooting. Running.

19.

Living room.

DEREK   I went running along the shore. This park.
               Old people. In tracksuits. Moving slowly. In
               unison. Felt like I was part of something.

MADDIE   Daddy. When're you coming home?

DEREK   Soon.

MADDIE   Do you want to see the routine? I've been
               practising.

DEREK   Not now darling. Work.

MADDIE   Is the weather nice there? How's the
               weather?

DEREK   Hot. When people come into the service
               station, they're hot and sweaty. Even at
               night. Sticky. Inside, it's air conditioned so I
               just sitting around freezing. Sometimes I go

	out by the pumps to warm up. Been helping Gloria with her lines?
MADDIE	Yep.
DEREK	Good girl.
	Silence.
	You would have loved it. All these old people in tracksuits moving in slow-motion.
GLORIA	I'm uncomfortable with the material.
DEREK	Synchronicity.
GLORIA	In my dreams, I'm her.
DEREK	Could have run forever. Under the palms. It's so frigging clean. You go to jail for spitting or sticking your gum under a bench.
GLORIA	I wake up tired. Like I spent the whole night underground. Can't face rehearsals.
DEREK	You'll be fine.
GLORIA	Just want to stay up here. Safe.
DEREK	Get Maddie to help with your lines. You're good at this.
GLORIA	An old man on the bus stared at me.
DEREK	He what?
GLORIA	Stared.
DEREK	Well he probably recognised you.
GLORIA	His eyes. Stripped me. His wrinkly body. Hot and sticky. Derek? Are you there? The connection's really. You're frozen.

20.

The Balcony.

CLIENT   What a view.

CASSIE   Yes.

CLIENT   Wow.

CASSIE   The lights. Boats.

CLIENT   That building there. See?

CASSIE   With the palm on the roof?

CLIENT   Yeah. They got a pool up there.

            Pause.

            I'm on the tenth floor. View's nothing like this. This is wow.

CASSIE   Can I get you a drink?

CLIENT   A drink. Yeah nice. Thank you.

21.

Living room.

DEREK   Am I still frozen? I'm moving my arms. Am I still frozen? Shit. Gloria? You're breaking up. All pixelated. Sweetheart? Now you're frozen. Shit.

22.

Bathroom.

CASSIE splashes water on her face.

CASSIE   I'm melting. Jesus. My last one was scary. Short bald guy. Stank of cigarettes. Asked if he had to wear a condom. About half

the men ask. I put it on him. Spun me
round. Hard. Against the mirror. I wasn't
expecting it. I was really fucking scared.
Never know. Which guy might end up being
unsafe.

Puts on lipstick.

Put my face on. Get back out there.

23.

Living room.

PAUL	Do you know where my mum is?
JARED	She went out.
PAUL	With one of her friends?
JARED	I don't know where she.
PAUL	Are you and my mum friends?
JARED	I don't really know her.
PAUL	Do you want to be her friend?
	Silence.
CASSIE	Make yourself comfortable.
CLIENT	I will thanks.
JARED	I only just met her.
PAUL	How come you're here?
JARED	I'm looking after you. I'm a neighbour.
PAUL	I don't know you.
CLIENT	I feel like we. Even though we only. Like I know you.
CASSIE	We've only just met.

CLIENT	This thing between us.
PAUL	How much is she paying you?
CLIENT	A bond.
JARED	Just. Normal rates.
CLIENT	Anything I'm not allowed to do?
CASSIE	Stay respectful and we'll be fine.
CLIENT	Can we kiss?
CASSIE	Yes you can kiss me.
CLIENT	I can? Really?
CASSIE	Sure. Go ahead.
CLIENT	Wow so it's not true that stuff in movies how the guy's in love with a working girl but she won't let him kiss her because she's saving her kisses for a man she hasn't even met yet but loves with every fibre of her being until *finally* she realises *oh shit wow* it's actually him after all – he's *the one* – the one she's been saving her kisses for, and when they finally kiss, wow it's the moment we've all been waiting for, after all the confusion, they found each other and it's absolute fucking magic.
CASSIE	You can kiss me. Really it's fine.
	They kiss.
JARED	Dead. Got shot. We watch in replay. A bullet hits him in the shoulder and jerks his body back. Next enters his skull. Blood sprays in the fluorescent air of the concrete bunker. He twirls slo-mo. Blood cloud billows. Dead.
DEREK	Fuck.

CASSIE	I do it for him.
CLIENT	I want to be your.
CASSIE	I want him to have a future.
GLORIA	I can't breathe.
DEREK	Fuck it.
CLIENT	Friends. Can we be friends?
PAUL	Wanna play?
JARED	No thanks. I'm fine.
CLIENT	Is everything okay? You seem a bit.
DEREK	I'm frozen. Fuck.
CASSIE	I'm fine.
CLIENT	Are you upset?
GLORIA	Help me. I can't.
CASSIE	No. No. I'm fine.
CLIENT	Aren't you enjoying?
CASSIE	I'm fine. It's good. Feels good.
DEREK	Fuck, fuck, fuck.
PAUL	You seem.
CLIENT	Not really here.
PAUL	Just sitting there.
CLIENT	Am I boring you?
PAUL	Can have a go. If you want.
CASSIE	I'm fine. Really.
JARED	I'm fine.
DEREK	Am I still frozen?

GLORIA	Help me please.
PAUL	Wanna play a game?
JARED	Said I'm fine.
PAUL	No I mean like a real game.
DEREK	My arms and legs are numb. Face numb. Frozen.

MADDIE twirls her ribbons.

Can't move. Stuck. Can't feel my face.

GLORIA	Are you listening?
CASSIE	I don't feel a thing.
PAUL	You count. I'll hide.
DEREK	Beautiful darling. Wow, getting good. Really coming along.
JARED	10 9 8 7 6 –
CLIENT	TV flickers. Mute. Can't believe she left it on. During.
JARED	Coming ready or not.
CLIENT	War. Concrete.
MADDIE	Been practising.
CLIENT	Dust and blood.
JARED	Coming to get you.
GLORIA	I don't know. If now's the right time. For.
CASSIE	He paid. Do what he wants.
DEREK	Please.
GLORIA	For us to. Me. I.

MADDIE	Want to go in a competition, feel that. Everyone cheering when you pull off a move.
CASSIE	It doesn't *mean* anything. It's a transaction.
DEREK	We *need*. For us.
CASSIE	Fake it.
GLORIA	If I can.
CLIENT	Chopper strafing. Slow mo. Miniature people. Falling.
GLORIA	Into the world.
DEREK	Please darling. Us.
GLORIA	Right now.
MADDIE	Can I Daddy? Please.
CLIENT	Pixels.
GLORIA	When are you coming home?
CASSIE	I do it for him. My son.
JARED	Paul. Paul.
	Silence.
	Okay Paul, you win. You can come out now.
	Silence.
	I looked everywhere.
CASSIE	What do you mean everywhere?
JARED	Gone. I can't find.
CASSIE	People don't. PAUL.
JARED	I looked everywhere. He's not.
CASSIE	He can't just disappear. People don't just.

MADDIE	I want the whole world looking at me twirling, spinning, leaping. I want them to roar with happiness.
CASSIE	He can't.
GLORIA	If I can.
MADDIE	Daddy.
GLORIA	Handle this.
DEREK	We're not allowed to leave the hotel.
GLORIA	With everything.
MADDIE	Where's Daddy?
GLORIA	Mexico.
DEREK	I'm in Mexico City, sweetheart. We're not allowed to leave the hotel. The insurance doesn't cover us if we're out in the city unprotected. Every morning we get escorted from the lobby by security and driven in shiny black vans to meetings in tall glass buildings in this area with other glass buildings where we teach protocols and installation procedures. We step them through the training materials, get the system running, then security bundles us in the vans, back to the hotel, safely inside in the lobby.
MADDIE	When's he coming?
GLORIA	Soon darling.
CASSIE	He can't just disappear.
JARED	He hid.
CASSIE	Hid?
JARED	He was hiding.

CASSIE	From you? Hiding from you?
DEREK	We kill time around the pool. Or watch Mexican soap operas in our rooms.
JARED	Yeah.
CASSIE	Why would he do that Jared? Why would a little boy want to hide from you?
MADDIE	Why doesn't he come home?
DEREK	I feel at home in the hotel. Anonymous. Flipping channels.
CASSIE	You're sick. You know that? Sick.
GLORIA	I'm freezing. Darling shut the door.
CASSIE	PAUL. PAUL. PAUL.
	Silence.
CLIENT	Is she even paying attention?
	Silence.
	I'm paying. I can do what I want.
CASSIE	I spoke to security. There's nothing on the surveillance. They checked the hallway. The entire floor. Elevators. Nothing. We looked everywhere. I told them. They said no way he left the apartment. They know – can see – who comes and goes. He's not on tonight's footage. They said he must still be in here. But we've looked and looked. Jesus. PAUL? PAUL? DARLING. YOU CAN COME OUT NOW. MUMMY'S HERE. MUMMY'S HOME. PLEASE BABY.
JARED	I was in the corner. Watching. I wasn't supposed to be there. They didn't want me there. She held a knife to his throat and with one clean slice, she cut his throat. Like this –

He demonstrates.

CASSIE	You fuck. You sick fuck.
CLIENT	Hey, calm.
JARED	Don't. Please don't.
CASSIE	How dare you.
CLIENT	Calm down.
JARED	Calm.
MADDIE	Where are you?
CASSIE	Do you have any idea what you've.
DEREK	I watch porn. Drink beer from the mini-bar.
CASSIE	How dare.
GLORIA	They want me to go back.
MADDIE	Come home.
DEREK	What?
GLORIA	They want me to go. Visit. The rooms where.
DEREK	Do you think that's a good?
JARED	With one clean. A slice. His little neck.
GLORIA	Where it happened. The cellar.
JARED	He drops into her arms. She lowers his body. Closes his eyes. Kisses his eyes.
CASSIE	*(Weeping.)* Come back. Please come back. Darling come back.
DEREK	Do you think that's a good.
GLORIA	My life.

JARED	She cradles him. He actually looks like me. Doesn't move.
MADDIE	The ribbons.
CLIENT	Afterwards. I feel sick.
GLORIA	I want this.
MADDIE	Twirling.
CLIENT	The forty or so seconds of the orgasm is the only bit that's any good. The rest – withdrawing money from the machine, the chit-chat, pumping someone who couldn't care less – makes me want to disappear. Afterwards I just drive. Empty streets. The smell of her.
MADDIE	Falling. Twirling.
CASSIE	Please.
GLORIA	Home.

25.

GLORIA's bedroom.

DEREK	Her hair's damp. Her nightgown clings to her skin. The house is quiet. Her breathing.
	Silence.
	My wife.

26.

Living room.

JARED	When did you get?
DEREK	It's corrective. My overbite.
JARED	Do you have any idea.

GLORIA	Jared. Leave him.
JARED	How frigging ridiculous you look, Derek?
DEREK	I got the clear ones. Ceramic. So they blend in.
JARED	Can't even talk properly.
MADDIE	How long do you have to wear them for?
DEREK	Two, two and a half years.
JARED	Have you heard yourself?
MADDIE	What are they for?
DEREK	They'll align and straighten daddy's teeth. For dental health.
JARED	Brace face.
DEREK	It's – a good step.
GLORIA	Jared. Grow up.
JARED	Metal mouth.
DEREK	Ceramic actually. They're ceramic.
MADDIE	Will I have to have braces?
GLORIA	I don't think so darling.
DEREK	These are from Mexico.

*He gives presents to Maddie and Jared.
Sombreros.*

A rather long silence.

DEREK	It's good for my career. Help me go places.
GLORIA	You're away all the time.
DEREK	I mean.
GLORIA	I know.

DEREK   Don't you want to kiss me?

               They kiss.

               Do they get in the way?

GLORIA   It's fine. I'll get used to it.

DEREK   Have you been thinking about?

GLORIA   Yes and I want to.

DEREK   Really? I thought you – really?

GLORIA   I think it'd be good for me.

DEREK   *Good for us.* I want this too.

GLORIA   I mean.

DEREK   Great, this is really great.

GLORIA   I'm talking about.

DEREK   Just what we need.

GLORIA   The show.

DEREK   Oh.

GLORIA   I meant the show.

               Silence.

               He flips channels on the television. Sound on
               mute. Cars on fire. You can hear the burning.
               Close. Down there. In the streets. Distorted.
               A slowed down howl.

               Silence.

               They want me to visit where she was kept.
               The actual rooms.

               Silence.

JARED   I place the shots where I like. The head. Or
               leg if I want them to fall first.

Silence.

GLORIA   Where he kept her. That pig. Rehearsals are tough. That fucking pig of a man. And Dominic. This tension. He knows I'm scared and he's pushing. Can't help himself. Like he wants to humiliate me. And well now there's this idea to visit the rooms. The actual cellar. Dominic thinks it might help. And the documentary. You know they're filming rehearsals right? There's a lot of interest in Dominic right now. In the project. In me. Anyway. They want to film me there. My reactions. Derek? Where he kept her. Her whole childhood. The monster.

DEREK   Can you believe this is happening? Can you believe this is happening here?

MADDIE   I stand on tippy toes and look down. Noise. Sirens. And this roar. Like an animal in pain. Things smashing. Burning.

DEREK   It's okay. We're safe up here. Jesus. Can you believe it?

GLORIA   Where's Jared?

MADDIE   He said to tell you he went out.

GLORIA   Fuck.

26.

Living room.

JARED   How's Paul?

CASSIE   Fine. With his father. Custody.

JARED   Down there?

CASSIE   I spoke to them. He's fine.

JARED	Are you scared?
CASSIE	We're safe up here.
	Pause.
	You can smell the burning.
JARED	Do you ever get.
CASSIE	What?
JARED	Lonely. When Paul's not here.
CASSIE	I miss him of course. He's my boy.
JARED	Do you sleep with people – men – for money?
	Pause.
CASSIE	Is that what?
JARED	I heard. Yes. That you.
CASSIE	I do it so.
JARED	Do you think we?
CASSIE	For his future. I'm sorry – what?
	Pause.
JARED	I saved up. From the babysitting.
CASSIE	Jared, I don't think.
JARED	I'm scared. The riots.
	Silence.
	My first. Please. With you.
	Silence.
CASSIE	You're a boy.
JARED	Can I kiss you?

CASSIE	Smoke. Noise.
	Pause.
	We're safe up here.
JARED	I have money.

27.

PAUL's room.

PAUL	I got lost. Went into a room. Mummy wasn't there. It wasn't our house but the stuff was the same. I called. She didn't come. No one. The TV. No sound. Men and women dancing. In circles. Everybody clapped. No sound. I called for my mummy.

28.

Living room.

GLORIA	Have you seen Jared?
MADDIE	No.
GLORIA	He's not in his room.
DEREK	He'll miss breakfast.
MADDIE	He hasn't slept at home for days.
GLORIA	What?
MADDIE	You didn't know?
GLORIA	Where is he?
MADDIE	Maybe he got a girlfriend. How would I know? Leave me alone.

29.

Living room.

PAUL comes in.

CASSIE	You shouldn't be here darling.
	Pause.
	You should be in bed sweetheart.
	Pause.
	Jared is visiting Mummy. He came to say hi to Mummy.
	Pause.
PAUL	I can't sleep. The noise.
CASSIE	We're safe up here.
PAUL	I had a bad dream.
CASSIE	I'll come tuck you in soon, sing you a song. Go to bed.
JARED	Paul. It's late. Go to bed.
	JARED kisses CASSIE. A deep kiss. PAUL just stares.

30.

Living room.

GLORIA	They want me to relive it.
DEREK	What?
GLORIA	The cellar. My reactions. So people.
	Silence.
	The documentary. I want to do it.
	Silence.

They're offering good.

DEREK   This is not about.

GLORIA   It's *generous.* And Dominic.

DEREK   It's never been about the.

GLORIA   You could be here more.

DEREK   I'm.

GLORIA   You wouldn't have to go away so much.

          Pause.

DEREK   If this is what you. If you think it's good.

GLORIA   The actual rooms. Where her father kept her.

DEREK   For you.

          Silence.

          Do you like my new teeth?

31.

CASSIE's room.

JARED   She's not porcelain. Her face isn't painted on. She's real. Like me. The noise from the streets doesn't wake her. She reaches for me in her sleep.

          She does.

          When I was a little, I used to watch my mother working. Rehearsals. Sometimes they kicked me out. *Grown up scenes.* But I snuck in. Watched from under a table or behind a piece of scenery. Once she was holding – cradling – this boy. He looked just like me. She held a kitchen knife to his neck.

He demonstrates.

And sliced. Clean. A slit. Now he was heavier. She lowered his body. Kissed his eyes. Calm. Full of love. Like a mother. I wanted to forget. I never forgot. She reaches in her sleep. From a dream. For me.

He strokes her face.

32.

Living room.

MADDIE	I want to talk to Daddy.
GLORIA	The time sweetheart.
MADDIE	I need to talk to him.
GLORIA	Time difference.
MADDIE	I need to ask him something. Important.
GLORIA	Were you asleep?
DEREK	Is everything?
GLORIA	Maddie wants to.
MADDIE	Needs.
GLORIA	To ask you.
MADDIE	When Mummy died did you still love her? Do you still love her?
DEREK	I.

Silence.

MADDIE   Gloria says nothing. Sits and stares. Frozen. Sometimes hours. Or repeats. Like she'll be telling me something or asking me how my day was and she just repeats how was your day like she never even asked the first time. Like she totally forgot.

PAUL   Mummy. The noise. I can't sleep.

MADDIE   Her hands shake. She tries to hide it.

PAUL   Will they take our TV? Will they smash our things?

MADDIE   One night, I got up to go to the loo. She was dancing. Alone. Holding her arms around herself. Like this –

She demonstrates.

Turning slowly. She didn't see me.

Silence. GLORIA dances. MADDIE watches.

DEREK   Is there anything you need? I can. There's this huge market here in an underground car-park. It's really bright. Handbags, shoes, sunglasses. You name it. The latest. And cheap. Gloria?

GLORIA   Music. Far away.

She dances.

DEREK   Gloria? Jesus. Thin air.

MADDIE   Daddy are you there?

DEREK dances with GLORIA. A slow shuffle.

GLORIA   Daddy.

Dancing.

PAUL   The noise.

JARED   Want to play a game?

PAUL   Mummy.

CASSIE   The view.

JARED	Yes.
CASSIE	Can see forever.
JARED	Yes. I kiss her neck. Soft.
	Pause.
	I want to join the fighting. Protect us. A soldier.
CASSIE	Jared. You.
	Pause.
	It's still burning.

33.

Living room.

DEREK	Where is everybody? MADDIE. MADDIE. Where's Maddie?
GLORIA	Why are you?
DEREK	Where is she?
GLORIA	Shouting.
DEREK	I looked in her room. Everywhere. Her ribbons. The balcony.
GLORIA	Stop shouting all the.
DEREK	I'M NOT SHOUTING. WHERE'S MADDIE? WHERE THE FUCK IS SHE?
GLORIA	Since when?
DEREK	WHERE?
GLORIA	When did you start being so?
DEREK	I'M LOUD OKAY AT THE FOOTBALL AT THE BAR CRACKING JOKES MY

MATES LOUD FUCKING LOUD I'M A
LOUD FUCKER. NOW WHERE'S MY
DAUGHTER?

GLORIA   We were watching TV. Dancing.

DEREK   ARE YOU DRUNK? JESUS. CAN'T
          LEAVE YOU ALONE. MADDIE.
          MADDIE.

GLORIA   A family again.

DEREK   Jesus. I can't.

GLORIA   Dominic yells at me. Now you. You never used.

DEREK   Jesus. The noise.

GLORIA   He doesn't believe in me. The role. But. At
          night. Down there. Cold. The walls. And
          music. The river. Muck. Those rooms.

35.

Street.

MADDIE   I heard the noise, saw the fires. The burning
          smell. And on TV. Windows smashed.
          People carrying stuff. Police. I stood on the
          balcony and didn't have that feeling I might
          jump. I wasn't afraid. We weren't allowed
          to go down but I wanted to see for myself.
          Security was protecting our building.
          Standing around. Watching their monitors.
          Didn't stop me. Like I was invisible. On TV
          they said that the looters were criminals.
          Animals. I wanted to see.

36.

The walls close in.

GLORIA   Is anyone there? Somebody. Please.

Silence.

Can you hear me? Please. Someone.

Silence.

Please. Please.

Silence.

Listen.

Silence.

The river.

Fade.

Two.

A room without windows.

GLORIA alone.

GLORIA   Back?

           Pause.

           Coming back here?

           Pause.

           Give me a moment.

           Silence.

           Okay.

           Pause.

           Coming back? How I feel coming here? It's –

           A girl of around 12 enters and stands beside GLORIA.
           She might be the young GLORIA.

           A long silence.

GIRL   You – you grew.

GLORIA   Yes. I'm grown up now.

           Silence.

GIRL   Do you still think about me?

GLORIA   Yes.

           Pause.

           Of course I do. Yes.

GIRL   Remember when we saw the sky? Huge and
           white. Remember?

GLORIA	It hurt my eyes.
GIRL	Yes. Can you hear the river?
GLORIA	No.
GIRL	Daddy says the river is ancient.

The girl has a doll. A baby. She makes it crawl around the room.

Mummy's little girl. We call her Maddie. Daddy and me. Hello Maddie.

GLORIA	Shhh.
GIRL	I feed her.
GLORIA	I don't want to.

Footsteps are heard on the ceiling.

GIRL	Daddy.

Silence. They listen. After a while a man enters. Sits. Reads a newspaper.

GLORIA	Do you know who I am?

Silence.

Don't you recognise?

Silence.

MAN	*(To the GIRL.)* What was that? Did you say something darling?
GIRL	How was your day?
MAN	Fine. Just fine.
GIRL	Did you walk along the river?
MAN	Not today darling. I was busy. All day.
GLORIA	No.

GIRL	Did you bring me something?
MAN	Like what?
GLORIA	I shouldn't be here.
GIRL	Something special.
GLORIA	I can't.
GIRL	A present.
GLORIA	I'm freezing.
GIRL	The river.
MAN	You can't have presents everyday.
GIRL	I know.
GLORIA	I'm sorry.
MAN	But since you were such a good girl looking after Maddie.
GIRL	Daddy!

He produces a small package wrapped in tissue paper and gives it to her.

GLORIA	The bird.

The GIRL opens it. A painted tin bird.

MAN	Do you?
GLORIA	It's beautiful. Thank you.
MAN	You squeeze the handle. The wings. To make it fly.

The GIRL does.

Like that.

GIRL	Thank you. I love it.
MAN	How's Maddie?

221

GIRL	She's good. We were –
GLORIA	Playing.

The MAN picks up the doll and plays with her, lifting her in the air above him, smiling and making faces.

MAN	*(To the doll.)* Hello little one. Say hello. My precious little girl. Hello Maddie.
GIRL	There's a house on top of ours. They had a little girl but she died. Now they're sad.
GLORIA	Why?
GIRL	She went out. It wasn't safe. She got lost.
MAN	What about you?
GIRL	I'm happy here, Daddy.
GLORIA	Where's Dominic? *(Screams.)* Dominic!

GLORIA hides her face and sobs. The GIRL is distressed.

Where's fucking Dominic?

MAN	Why don't you go to your room darling? Take Maddie, read her a story.

The GIRL leaves with the doll.

Can't you see you're upsetting her, Gloria.

Pause.

Gloria?

GLORIA sobs.

Calm.

MAN	Jesus Gloria. You stink of booze.
GLORIA	I'm –
MAN	Fuck's sake.

GLORIA	What? What?
MAN	Get a grip.
GLORIA	I'm fine.
MAN	I believe in you. Dominic does too. What you're doing here is brave.
GLORIA	I feel fake. Air. A window. Jesus.
MAN	What's there to see?
GLORIA	What if she?
MAN	What?
GLORIA	Wants to see.
MAN	See what? You have no idea.
GLORIA	The world.
MAN	Do you have any idea how dangerous it is out there. Drugs. Scum. Men who want to hurt her. She's safe here. We're a family. Happy.

The GIRL enters.

She practices with her ribbon.

MAN	Hey that's coming along.
GIRL	Been practising.
MAN	Good.

She practices. He watches.

GIRL	Is she okay?
MAN	All better now.
GIRL	All better.

Silence.

GIRL   You like it?

GLORIA   What?

The GIRL shows her the ribbon.

GIRL   My ribbon. Daddy gave it to me. I'm
                  learning a routine.

GLORIA   I remember.

GIRL   Daddy gave it me.

She twirls the ribbon.

GLORIA   You're getting good. *(Correcting.)* Gave me
                  it.

GIRL   You have to keep the ribbons moving. Not
                  allowed to stop. This is *twirl* and this is
                  spiral and this one *snake* and *loop the loop.*
                  Look – *flowers.*

*She performs her routine. The MAN's phone rings. He
leaves. Sound of a door being locked. Sound of someone
moving upstairs. Then silence, the ribbons.*

GLORIA   You don't have to do that. With the ribbons.
                  Just to please him.

The GIRL slows the ribbons down.

You don't have to believe his stories. It's stuff
he makes up. To keep you here.

*The GIRL stops and listens, ribbons hanging, head
bowed.*

The world isn't a prison. It's glorious. And
you're part of it.

The sound of something being dragged upstairs.

The river isn't polluted. It's not filled with
muck and animals. It's a normal brown

river flowing from the mountains to the sea.
Through our city where it's broad and gentle.
The people who founded our city decided
his was a good place to live. Fresh water
for drinking, washing clothes, swimming.
Fishing, boats, trade. You should see the
river on a summer afternoon. It's glorious.
Like everything might dissolve. Or on foggy
mornings when people crossing bridges are
ghosts. Or night. Alone. The lights. Rippling.

The GIRL trembles with fear or excitement.

The sky is vast. It hangs. Like a sheet. Eye.
Egg. You feel it. Humming. You stand on
a bridge and watch the water transporting
memories and dreams. You feel small. Part of
a gigantic world.

Sound of faraway music. The MAN returns.

(To the MAN.) Do you remember me?

Silence. The music. The MAN ignores her.

Don't you recognise me?

*Silence. The music. The GIRL crosses to the man and
takes his hand.*

I remember.

*The MAN and the GIRL dance a slow waltz. GLORIA
watches. They dance like this until the music stops.
The GIRL holds the MAN. He doesn't move. Something
wooden and stiff about how he stands. Like a
marionette.*

GIRL   I want to go outside.

Silence. The GIRL hugging the MAN.

MAN   It's not safe.

GIRL	Maddie wants to see the river.
MAN	How do you know?
GIRL	She told me.
MAN	She can't talk.
GIRL	She wants to walk in the sun.
MAN	The river's dirty.
GIRL	It's not, it's not.
MAN	Foul. Baby carriage, dead horse, bloated. Filth.
GIRL	No.

Silence. The GIRL trembles.

MAN	What about Maddie.

The GIRL looks at the doll.

Let me go.

She lets him go.

Doll.

She picks up the doll.

Wall.

She walks to the wall.

Face.

She faces the wall.

We're lucky. We don't need anyone.

GLORIA spits in the MAN's face. He doesn't react, doesn't wipe it away.

GIRL	*(Still facing wall.)* Lucky.

MAN	Perfect life.
GIRL	Perfect.
MAN	No one will ever harm you.
GLORIA	Disgusting. Pig. Animal. I hate you.
	She attacks the MAN, hits him, claws at him, but he doesn't react.
	Sick sick pig. You sick fucking pig.
GIRL	*(Still facing wall.)* Leave Daddy alone. Stop it. You're hurting him.
GLORIA	You monster.
	GLORIA attacks him. He's completely impassive. Slowly, with a minimum of effort, he gains control and holds her until she exhausts herself. The GIRL stands against the wall. The doll hanging from her hand.
GLORIA	Let me go.
	He releases GLORIA.
GLORIA	I'm. I can't. I'm sorry –
	She leaves the room. Silence. The GIRL relaxes, i.e. stops facing the wall.
MAN	You okay darling?
GIRL	I'm okay.
MAN	It's a tough scene. I know.
GIRL	I'm okay. What're we doing now?
MAN	I think we're taking some kind of a break.
GIRL	Is she okay?
MAN	She'll be fine. She's all wound up. The role.
	The MAN's phone rings.

MAN	Just a second, darling.
	He answers it as he leaves. The GIRL is left alone. She plays with the doll.
GIRL	It's okay. Mummy's here.
	Another MAN, wearing an earpiece enters, whispers to the GIRL. They leave together. She leaves the doll lying on the floor. After some time, another WOMAN enters. Dressed like GLORIA.
WOMAN	By myself yes no intimacy prefer alone yes of course I think about him every day mostly gentle kind sometimes funny yes he told me stories presents great with the children a real joker great dad of course I cried when I heard he was dead I have a heart knew they were hunting him panicked strange in front of a train I always imagined him drowning in that filthy river bloated shame yes I fantasied about killing him sawing his head off you saw where I lived on TV right cold damp disgusting no windows fluoro light preserved alive Nerfertiti stuck awake wondering what happens if he dies I die nobody knows and my children what about them sometimes yes he let me upstairs curtains always drawn booby-trapped he said we lived a normal life I cooked cleaned watched TV looked after the babies we didn't need anyone he said no one to harm me yes sent back under when visitors came he wiped every surface not just to hide traces of me he was obsessed order cleanliness bind my hair with clips wear the plastic shower cap to catch stray hairs shave myself bald saying for hygiene not allowed to cry never because salt traces DNA then he choked me head under water for example fingerprint

on glass once I stole a look through the
curtains sky bright so bright then yes the end
the garage on knees cleaning car his phone
rang because the vacuuming was loud off he
walked took my chance jumped gate ran ran
ran climbing fences calling help police please
no one stopped only that one lady brought
me in the police the medical I said save my
children please on television they said the
children were speaking a made up language
like animals I remember flashes cameras
outside the station yes I read the headlines
victim stamped on my head no I almost
never go out my favourite activity is reading
plus breeding cacti taking photos I prefer
inside glasses on a table a few leaves from the
philodendron over there –

She points. There is no pot plant.

The way light falls in a room, details.

*She leaves the room. The room is empty. Distant
music. At last, the GIRL enters and plays with the doll.
The MAN comes in and sits, watches her play. GLORIA
enters dressed in her underwear. Eyes red from crying.
Or glycerine. The MAN wearing the earpiece follows
her in, stands in corner.*

MAN 2   Good. Okay.

              GLORIA sits.

              A few close-ups.

GLORIA   Sitting or?

MAN 2   That's good.

              He listens to the earpiece.

              Okay Gloria. He wants to hear the new text.
              The *shattered speech*. Her interior.

229

She just stares.

Gloria?

GLORIA   Okay.

MAN 2   Remember what he said? You heard him. He believes in you.

GLORIA   Yes.

MAN 2   Her story. The shattered.

The MAN with the earpiece withdraws.

GLORIA   Yes.

Long silence.

Think flesh sky yes blood ribbon bird.

She sits with eyes closed.

Open clean help.

The GIRL leaves the doll and picks up the tin bird.

Crawl wall music baby spit cold river white.

MAN   Good.

GLORIA   Face hole sky.

The GIRL makes the tin bird fly.

MAN   Good. That's good. Do it again.

Will she?

Fade.

Three.

Theatre dressing room.

DEREK	Do you like my teeth?
JARED	What?
DEREK	My new teeth.
JARED	Nice. Must've cost.
DEREK	You know.
JARED	Cosmetic.
DEREK	Corrective.
JARED	Oh. Right.
DEREK	Do you like them?
JARED	Derek. They're not exactly new.
DEREK	I know but I'm asking if.
JARED	Brace face.
DEREK	Okay.
JARED	Metal mouth.
DEREK	Porcelain.
JARED	Whatever.
DEREK	Porcelain and plastic.
JARED	Whatevs.
DEREK	Blends in.
JARED	Does it?
DEREK	My wife likes them.

JARED	*(Sarcastic.)* Your wife.
DEREK	Anyway. My bite needed correcting.
JARED	Ever get food stuck?
DEREK	Food what?
JARED	In between.
DEREK	What? No. Sometimes.
JARED	I met this girl in the bar. After show last night. Ohmyfuckinggod.
DEREK	Hot?
JARED	What?
DEREK	Hot, was she hot?
JARED	Yes she was hot.
DEREK	And?
JARED	And what nothing. She dug the show. Thought it was edgy.
DEREK	Did she like my work?
JARED	She didn't really mention you.
DEREK	Okay.
JARED	Not specifically.
DEREK	But she liked the show?
JARED	She did.
DEREK	Great. That's great.
JARED	Actually, she liked your teeth.
DEREK	What?
JARED	Yeah. She loved them. Your metal smile.

DEREK	Porcelain. Did she?
JARED	No, no she didn't.
DEREK	Right.
JARED	She asked me to sign her programme, blinking her fuck-me-eyes.
DEREK	No way.
JARED	Yes way. She eye-fucked me.
	He demonstrates.
DEREK	Jesus wept.
JARED	Yup.
DEREK	And?
JARED	And – weirdest thing – when she was sucking my dick she kept saying your name.
DEREK	She what?
JARED	Over and over. 'Derek, Derek.' Looking up. Mouth full. 'Derek. You're magnificent.'
DEREK	What? She didn't?
JARED	No she did not.
DEREK	Right.
JARED	*(Pretending to have a full mouth.)* 'Derek… Oh Derek… Your teeth are perfect.'
DEREK	Ha-dee-fucking-ha.
JARED	Apparently Gloria doesn't want to go on.
DEREK	When does she?
JARED	She's in a foul mood.
DEREK	When is she not?

JARED	Is it true you and she once?
DEREK	What? Who?
JARED	Gloria. I heard.
DEREK	Well.
	Slight pause.
JARED	Naughty naughty Derek.
DEREK	Once. A long time ago.
JARED	Dirty dog.
DEREK	We've been friends since drama school.
JARED	And?
DEREK	She's like a sister.
JARED	Oh you sick puppy.
DEREK	Not like that. Jesus.
JARED	And?
DEREK	What?
JARED	So?
DEREK	So what?
JARED	Did you bang her brains out?
DEREK	We were both pretty drunk.
JARED	I bet she was wild back then.
DEREK	I don't.
JARED	A stone cold fox.
DEREK	She's.
JARED	And? Now? Would you go there?
DEREK	I don't know, she's.

JARED	Pretty fucking crazy right.
DEREK	Having a rough time.
JARED	She's fucking mental right?
DEREK	Jared.
JARED	And drunk. Always drunk. Man.
DEREK	Don't talk about her like.
JARED	She used to be so amazing. Incredible. I'd do her though.
DEREK	What?
JARED	Even though she's old.
DEREK	Whoa hang-on she's hardly *old*.
JARED	C'mon, she's a total fucking MILF.
DEREK	Christ.
JARED	Pretty fucking wild. Am I right? Take me there Derek. Blow by blow.
DEREK	I'm not.
JARED	Wide screen, slow mo, uncut. Please Uncle Derek.
DEREK	Grow up.
JARED	She's still got a banging body.
DEREK	And?
JARED	She's got the hots for me is what.
JDEREK	Right.
JARED	What?
DEREK	I said right as in uh-huh my friend don't think so.

JARED	Are you a teeny bit jealous Derek?
DEREK	As if.
JARED	I've seen how she looks at me.
	MADDIE enters.
DEREK	Jesus. You actually believe that every man, woman and child.
JARED	Um.
DEREK	Wants to jump your skinny bones and fuck your silly brains out.
JARED	Derek.
DEREK	What?
JARED	Um.
DEREK	What you big stud?
	He sings something sexy. Makes sexy moves in JARED's face.
JARED	Maddie.
	DEREK sees MADDIE.
DEREK	Oh. Hi.
MADDIE	Hi Derek.
DEREK	Did she?
JARED	Yep.
DEREK	Fuck.
MADDIE	Swear jar.
DEREK	Double fuck.
MADDIE	Pay up Daddy-O. Four bucks.
DEREK	Four? I only said three fucks.

MADDIE	Okay now it's five. The F-word thrice plus the double F-word.
DEREK	Jesus.
	He pays her.
	You been warming up Maddie?
MADDIE	Yeah you should try it sometime. Might help.
JARED	Did you see Gloria out there?
MADDIE	In the corridor. She's said she's not going on.
DEREK	She what?
MADDIE	Kip's talking to her. She's drunk.
DEREK	Maddie.
MADDIE	She can't even stand up properly. Plus she refuses to wear her wig. Kip says she has to. She says no f-ing way and now she's not going on. He tells she looks amazing in it. That the wig – actually, he says *hairpiece* – is a key to her character. She tells him to go f-ing f-himself. Kip's trying to stay calm but you can tell he's totally stressed. He turned scarlet. Have we had the half?
DEREK	Yep.
	MADDIE does her vocal warm up. Stretches etc.
JARED	Do you like Derek's new teeth?
MADDIE	Yeah sure they're fine.
DEREK	Thanks sweetheart.
JARED	Had an audition today.
DEREK	What for?

JARED	This 3D apocalypse thing, it's bullshit.
MADDIE	Kerching.

MADDIE puts her hand out. JARED pays her.

JARED	Wait.

He gives her another dollar.

Seriously, it's *fucking* stupid. The Earth's been completely destroyed and New York's a –

He gives her another dollar.

Total fucking wasteland. Lawless. Gangs, mutants, terror. Fucking mayhem.

She puts out her hand.

Wait. Anyway, I'm part of this unit that's gone AWOL because we don't believe in the corruption and overall bad decision making that has basically become fucking rampant in the what's left of the armed forces. We want to put things right, get ourselves out of this god awful fucking shit hole and make our way to California where there's still hope.

DEREK	Sorry what?
JARED	Hope. I said hope.
DEREK	What do you mean by hope?
JARED	Well, California is kinda okay, I mean compared to New York City, it's fucking paradise.

She puts out her hand.

I said wait, kiddo. People in Cali are on top of things, there's no chaos, sickness, mutants. In fact there's this big fuck-off fence separating the Free State of California from the rest of the US. There's me and the other guys in my unit plus this woman and kid and we're all trying to get to California. We're up to our necks in violence and desperation and mayhem – *the shit* – just trying to make it through each fucking day. To stay full of courage, free and alive. Anyway, the scene I did today, it's pretty bullshit. Some kind of flashback. I'm showering. Washing off blood. In a white-tiled room. These other guys are showering too. Soldiers. Guys my age plus old guys too. Maybe it's the start of the war, they didn't say. Anyway, my character is washing blood off. He's covered in gore. He sees the other guys through the steam scrubbing blood off their bodies too. It's like part of the daily routine. But it's as if he's seeing it for the first time. He doesn't want to end up like the old guys. Doesn't want to be stuck here fighting this goddam war for whatever fucking reason. The old guys are a premonition. The future he doesn't want to be part of. He wants out. That's fucking it. He's going AWOL. To California and freedom. How much?

MADDIE   Sixteen.

JARED   *(Pays her.)* Twenty and I want credit.

DEREK   And?

JARED   And what?

DEREK   How did you go?

JARED   Wasn't feeling it. And the director, I don't think he liked my choices.

DEREK   Damn bro.

JARED	Hey Maddie, there's a good role for you. This kid, this girl, she's like on the run disguised as a boy because it's safer for her like that. You should read for it.
MADDIE	My agent already discussed it with me. We don't think it's right for me. Anyway I don't want to do clichéd work. I only want to do work that's got integrity.
	Pause.
	What if she doesn't go on? Will they cancel?
DEREK	She'll go on.
MADDIE	All those people lining up to see her.
DEREK	Us. See us.
JARED	They want to see her fuck up. Forget her lines. Fall on her face. Total meltdown.
DEREK	Jared.
MADDIE	*(Robot voice.)* You have three swear credits remaining.
JARED	It's true. They love a catastrophe.
MADDIE	*(Robot voice.)* Top up now at wwwdotmaddierulesdotcom.
DEREK	You should cut her some slack.
JARED	She doesn't even *talk* to us anymore. You're supposed to be her old friend and when was the last time she even said boo to you? She's always pacing the corridors or outside chain smoking, refusing to go on. And who knows what she'll say or do when she does go onstage? It's not the script. It's not what we agreed on. What would Dominic think?
DEREK	Dominic's not here.

JARED	Hey Maddie. Fuckity fuck her and her fucking *hair-piece.*
MADDIE	*(Robot voice.)* You have zero dollars credit and zero dollars my bonus swear credit.
JARED	I don't think he'd like it much. What she's doing. What she's turning his play into. She never listens to Kip.
DEREK	As if Kip can give her notes.
JARED	Kip's notes are good.
DEREK	They're fine. I like Kip don't get me wrong but c'mon she was never going to take notes from him. She barely listens to Dominic.
MADDIE	They call him the Sphinx.
DEREK	What? Who?
MADDIE	Kip. The Sphinx.
DEREK	Who does?
MADDIE	Alice and Dominic.
JARED	Why?
MADDIE	Because of how he sits there. So serious.
DEREK	How do you know?
MADDIE	Alice told me. I think it's meant to be a compliment.
DEREK	Does he know?
MADDIE	Uh-uh. No way.
	MADDIE goes out.
JARED	I'm sick of her.
DEREK	Who? Maddie? Why?

JARED	What? No. Gloria.
DEREK	Right.
JARED	She makes it hard for me to go out there and be truthful.
DEREK	Look, sure it's been difficult lately.
JARED	She makes my blood freeze.
	Pause.
DEREK	You should have seen her when she was young. Dangerous. My god. You never knew what she'd do next. Really incredible.
JARED	The one where she kills her son.
DEREK	Okay. Medea.
JARED	Was it? Anyway whatever. In-fucking-credible.
DEREK	You saw that?
JARED	The film.
DEREK	Right.
JARED	The way she held the knife. And his little body. Her eyes. So full of love. That shit blew my mind.
	MADDIE returns.
JARED	She doesn't like them looking at her.
DEREK	Who?
JARED	The audience.
DEREK	What?
JARED	She actually says *why are they always staring at me*?

DEREK	It's some kind of breakdown.
JARED	Breakdown? She's a fucking train wreck.
MADDIE	Kerching.

He pays up.

Actually do you guys mind keeping it down. I'm trying to get in the zone.

She goes out again.

DEREK	*(Softly.)* I never actually.
JARED	What?
DEREK	We never.
JARED	Whoa what are you saying?
DEREK	That night. We.
JARED	Hold on. What night?
DEREK	When we. She and I. Too drunk. Nervous or whatever.
JARED	But everyone.
DEREK	I know but it's not true.
JARED	Jesus Derek. Jesus fucking. You never?
DEREK	No.
JARED	Oh you poor fuck. You mean she. You're in bed with her and.
DEREK	Right. No.
JARED	Oh man. Derek. You were like my hero for about five minutes. I *idolised* you. Because back then she must have been the greatest fuck on earth. Oh Derek. No wonder deep down you're so fucking sad.

DEREK	She's a star, still a star, every inch a star.
JARED	She's mean and washed up.
DEREK	You don't get it.
JARED	A shadow of her former.
DEREK	She's still got it.
JARED	Bullfuckingshit.
DEREK	They can't take their eyes off her. She's part of them. An embodiment of their innermost selves. However fucked up she gets, however much the wheels fall off. Out there. Every night. Lining up for tickets. Because of her. We're nothing. She's burnt into their minds. Her Nina, her Hedda, her Gertrude, her Clytemnestra, her whoever. She puts it all out there. Her love, her rage, her longing, her selfishness, her ecstasy, her glory, her squalor, her sorrow, her ferocity.
JARED	Anything you've forgotten, Dirk?
DEREK	Her perversity, her *courage*, the child she once was, her great wit, every inch of her sexual being, her wounds, her scars, her endless fucking struggle not to collapse into the abyss.
	Silence.
JARED	Nice.
DEREK	What?
JARED	Nice speech. No really. It was actually very moving.
DEREK	One day, you'll tell your grandchildren you worked with her.
JARED	*(Laughs.)* My what?

244

DEREK   That you were lucky enough to share a stage
             with her for a few hours of your pathetic,
             made-for-TV existence. You fluff.

JARED   Sorry, what did you just call me?

DEREK   Fluff. You piece of fluff.

JARED   Ouch Derek.

             He feigns hurt. MADDIE enters.

MADDIE   Why's Jared crying?

JARED   *(Through tears.)* He called me fluff.

MADDIE   Jesus Derek. That's not very sensitive.

             *She leaves again. She can't keep still. A bundle of
             nerves.*

DEREK   Washed up. What would you know? Bred
             on video games and porn and bullshit 3D
             zombie.

JARED   Mutant.

DEREK   Mutant meaningless fucking junk and you
             think you have the right to pass judgement
             on her. On her performance.

             MADDIE returns. Loud vocal warm-up.

             Her career. Her *life*? What do you
             know? About life? About being an artist?
             Lightweight.

MADDIE   Who's lightweight?

DEREK   Jared.

JARED   Moi.

MADDIE   Whoa.

JARED   Fuck you Derek. I'm sick of you and your
             whole generation. Everything you did was
             so much better, so important. So *radical*.
             You did it all. And what's left for us?
             Crumbs. Endless copies. The facsimiles of
             your great invention. Well fuck you. You
             has-been.

             MADDIE laughs.

             Your world makes me sad. You're a pack of
             self-obsessed, stagnant, fake as fuck cunts.

MADDIE   Whoa.

JARED   Your world is dead and your precious
             fucking theatre is dead.

             PAUL wanders in and sits down. Listens.

             A pathetic fucking joke.

PAUL   What's a joke?

JARED   This. Theatre. Fakery. Lies.

PAUL   Oh.

             Pause.

MADDIE   Don't say that. Jared. Please don't.

             Pause.

             I like it here. I like being with you guys. I
             like going onstage. Everyone watching. It
             makes me feel alive.

             Silence.

             By the way you owe the swear jar for five
             f-words and one c-word. Double for those
             uttered in reach of Paul's tender ears.

PAUL	Is it true we're not going on tonight? Will they send everyone away?
DEREK	We'll see mate.
JARED	A star. Burning out. Going going gone.
	An announcement over the tannoy: 'Ladies and gentlemen, this is your five minute call. You have five minutes until beginners.'
DEREK	Sounds like we're going on.
JARED	Does it?
	Silence. KIP enters.
DEREK	Hey, it's The Kipper. Whaddup bro?
JARED	Hey Kipster.
MADDIE	Kip are we going on?
KIP	Sure thing, Maddie.
PAUL	Cool.
	He wanders out.
JARED	Really?
KIP	Look we had a bit of a situation but it's sorted now so yeah.
MADDIE	Is she gonna wear the wig?
DEREK	Maddie.
KIP	Look I can't say.
DEREK	Got any notes for me?
KIP	What? Now?
DEREK	From last time?
KIP	You sure you want them now?

DEREK	It's okay. You in tonight dude?
KIP	Sure. Yep. Sure.
DEREK	Okay great. That's great. So notes?
KIP	Yep. Sure. Fine.
DEREK	Heard from Dominic? How is he?
KIP	Good. Having a good time.
JARED	Lucky guy.
DEREK	How about like a *general note.* Something overall to aim for tonight?
MADDIE	Guys please, a bit of shh around here.
DEREK	Sorry.

KIP's phone rings. An absurd ring tone.

KIP	Hi Dom… Yeah… I talked to her… Look maybe if you… Okay, fine… Yep, I'm with them now… Everyone Dominic says hi.
ALL	Hi Dominic.
KIP	What sorry you're breaking up… He says he misses you and thinks about you every time you're doing a show… He calculates the time difference… Yeah I told them… Maddie's fine. Right?
MADDIE	Yep.
DEREK	Can I?
KIP	Sorry Derek, what?
DEREK	Can I have a quick word? Kip? With Dominic?
KIP	Really?… Okay be quick.

DEREK	Hi Dom… Sure man okay… *(Sings in a techno robot voice.)* *'I'm bigger and badder and rougher and tougher, in other words sucker there is no other I'm the one and only Dominator…'* Yeah good man, good… How is it there?..
	Pause.
	Right… Fuck… Wow… Sounds incredible.
	He makes a 'sorry' face to Maddie, throws her a coin.
	Oh nothing really just wanted to ask if there was anything like advice, I'm feeling a bit you know stale and wanted to know if you had any special piece of advice, like a reminder or *key word,* you've been gone for ages and Kip's great but I'd really appreciate some –
	Pause.
	Right… Gotcha… Yeah I can do that… Ha… Yeah why not… Thanks man… Yeah you too… Here's Kip…
	He hands the phone back to KIP.
KIP	Yep yep okay…
	He passes the phone to JARED.
JARED	Hey Dom.
	Silence. JARED listens. After some time, he passes the phone back to KIP.
KIP	He's gone.
DEREK	What did he say?
JARED	Maddie block you ears.
MADDIE	What? Why?

JARED	Block them.
	She does.
	He said I should go out there and absolutely fucking destroy her.
	Silence. DEREK repeatedly opens and closes his mouth, part of his warm up. JARED leaves the room.
MADDIE	*(Too loud.)* Can I unblock my ears now?
DEREK	*(Nods.)* Yes sweetheart.
KIP	Have a good show guys.
DEREK	Thanks Kipster. Notes.
KIP	Later.
DEREK	Thanks bro.
MADDIE	Bye Kip.
	Silence.
	He's gone.
DEREK	The Sphinx. *(A funny voice.)* The Riddle of the Sphinx.
	He laughs too loud.
	(Again.) The Riddle of the Sphinx.
MADDIE	*(Confused.)* What?
DEREK	You know. The Sphinx.
MADDIE	What're you talking about?
DEREK	You know who the Sphinx is, right?
MADDIE	Sure. Kip.
DEREK	No. The actual Sphinx. Outside Thebes, beyond the gates, there's this statue in the desert. Huge. Face half gone. No one

remembers who carved it. Haunches of a lion, wings of a great bird, a woman's face. Anyone who wants to pass into Thebes has to answer her riddle or she strangles him and eats him.

MADDIE	Why do you say him?
DEREK	What?
MADDIE	Him. Why *him*? What if the traveller's a woman?
DEREK	Well in the story.
MADDIE	I bet I could answer the riddle. Bet the Sphinx would let me through.

GLORIA enters.

GLORIA	We're going on.

She goes into another smaller room. (Her private dressing room.)

MADDIE	*(A whisper.)* Do you think she'll wear it?
DEREK	*(Whisper.)* What?
MADDIE	*(Whisper.)* The wig.
DEREK	*(Whisper.)* No idea.

Silence.

MADDIE	Derek?
DEREK	Yes sweetheart?
MADDIE	Can we run my lines? The speech where I run away.
DEREK	Okay. But quick. We don't have much time.
MADDIE	*(At a lick.)* I didn't know if anyone was following me. I just ran. People everywhere.

Carrying TVs. Bags of stuff. Smashing shop windows, burning cars. I wasn't scared. It was *wild*. The sky was huge.

DEREK   Vast.

MADDIE   The sky was vast. A milky eye. Watching me run. The city burned. I thought someone would stop me, ask where was I going but they didn't, not even the police. I'd never seen so many people. When I got to the river, it was on fire too. I stood on the bridge with everyone. Watching the river burn. I thought now anything is possible. A whole new life. How was that?

DEREK   Great. Spot on. You know it.

MADDIE   Thanks.

Announcement: 'Ladies and gentleman, this is your beginner's call. This is your call to the stage.'

Here goes nothing.

DEREK   Have a good show.

MADDIE   Thanks you too.

They leave. Empty room. Silence. The hum of an audience is heard over the tannoy. After a while, GLORIA emerges from her smaller, private room. She has the wig on. She checks herself in a mirror.

GLORIA   Christ.

She leaves. Empty room. Audience hum. Nothing for a while. Then, MADDIE runs back into the room. She forgot her ribbons. She picks them up from her dressing table. Takes a few deep breaths. Shakes her limbs. Stops. Looks in a mirror.

MADDIE   You've got a dream, protect it. You want something, go get it.

Runs out again. The empty dressing room. CASSIE
passes through. Stretching.

CASSIE   *(Quietly speed-running lines.)* I put on my face.
Sit at the mirror. Eyes. Lips. Colour my
cheeks. I'm always like this. Before a date.
You know. Butterflies. What type of man.
What am I in for.

PAUL enters.

Let's go buster. High-five.

They high-five.

Alright.

They leave. The audience hum stops. Silence. Then
JARED's voice can be heard on the tannoy.

JARED'S VOICE   At night when I can't sleep, I walk through
the rooms. Feet on the carpet. The
refrigerator hums. Our house is a stage
set and I'm the only living character. The
others are puppets. Faces painted on.

GLORIA enters. Under the following strips and puts
on a gold sequin dress.

They lie in bed attached to strings. Snoring,
mumbling, farting. Until the string jerks and up
they get to play their parts.

She stares at herself in a dressing room mirror.

Removes wig.

She laughs silently or is she crying?

She can't stop.

Fade.

Four.

1.

Empty room.

JARED   I walk into this room I thought was empty.
Routine check. I don't see her immediately.
In a corner. Hands over head. Protecting.
As if like that she'd be invisible. As if we
might not see her and leave her alone. Like
that. Trembling.

*GLORIA, wearing a torn gold sequin dress, in the
corner. She looks the worse for wear.*

Dressed for a ball. Like a queen.

He helps her up.

This all happened years ago. I brought her
home. Made her my wife.

She can hardly stand. He stops her from falling.

That's it. Try and stand. Gloria, stand up.
That's it. Stay up. Good.

2.

Living room.

CASSIE is brushing PAUL's hair.

CASSIE   You look nice for when Mummy comes
home.

PAUL   Ow.

CASSIE   Nearly done. Good.

She finishes. He sits on the sofa. She brings him a glass of milk. He drinks.

You've got a milk moustache.

She laughs. He wipes his mouth with his sleeve. Sound of door being opened.

That must be.

PAUL   Mummy.

JARED enters carrying shopping bags.

JARED   Is she?

CASSIE   Not yet.

JARED   Been a good boy for Cassie? Did he behave?

CASSIE   An angel.

JARED   A present. For her premiere.

He shows her a dress.

CASSIE   Wow. It's.

Pause.

JARED   Why don't you.

CASSIE   She'll be back any.

JARED   Try.

She tries the dress on. He helps her with the zipper.

And the shoes.

He takes a pair of heels from a shopping bag.

CASSIE   I.

She puts them on.

JARED   Wow.

> *She walks around, a bit wobbly in the shoes. Looks at herself in a mirror.*
>
> You look absolutely.

CASSIE   I should really take it off.

JARED   Fucking amazing.

> *He stands behind her and kisses her neck. They look at themselves in the mirror. PAUL is watching.*

3.

Living room.

JARED folds the dress, puts it and the shoes back in the bags.

JARED   *(To PAUL.)* Where's Mummy?

> *Pause.*

Where's she got to?

> *Pause.*

How about the zoo this weekend? With dad? Check out the bird show?

> *Pause.*

It's incredible. Man, the hawks. You should see. And these wedge-tailed eagles which swoop right over you. Whoosh. This huge eagle. Pick you up with his talons and whoosh.

> *Pretending to be an eagle, he picks PAUL up and flies him around. Puts him down. PAUL straightens his hair, makes himself neat.*

What's up champ? You're quiet. Mum'll be home soon.

PAUL   I want to tell her.

JARED	Tell her what mate?
PAUL	About today. What happened.
JARED	Don't think that's a good.
PAUL	With Cassie.
	Silence.
	It was fun.
JARED	What?
PAUL	With Cassie. We made a cubby. She put spooky music on and we hid.
JARED	You won't say anything, will you? To Mummy.
PAUL	I want to go to the bird show. I want to see the eagle. Swooping.
JARED	We will mate. You and me. Daddy's gonna take a shower now. Okay?
PAUL	Yep.

5.

Bathroom.

JARED in shower.

JARED	At work. The showers. White tiled room. Dirty work. Steam. Blood. Hair, nails. Pink on the tiles. When will it be over? Old guys, naked and wrinkled in the steam. Don't want to *be them.* Don't recognise my face. I'm leaving her. I can't stay with her. Sick.

257

6.

Living room.

GLORIA   What's this?

JARED   It's for.

GLORIA   A dress.

JARED   For your premiere.

                She tries it on.

GLORIA   Can you. The zipper.

                He does.

JARED   You look.

GLORIA   Old.

JARED   Beautiful. As the day we. Try the shoes.

                She does. Stands in front of a mirror.

                Suits you.

                He stands behind her.

GLORIA   Thank you.

                He kisses her neck.

                You smell nice. You showered.

JARED   How was?

GLORIA   Didn't you shower at work? You always.

JARED   It was a rough day. And you? How was today? Better?

GLORIA   Do you feel guilty? Is the dress?

JARED   A what?

She takes the dress off. Stands in underwear. Unsteady.

GLORIA   You stink of her and you stink of blood.

JARED   Not in front.

GLORIA   Fucking stinks.

              She tears the dress.

JARED   Stop.

PAUL   Mummy.

JARED   Paul go to your.

PAUL   Mummy.

              PAUL clings to GLORIA.

PAUL   It's alright Mummy... Mummy...

GLORIA   Animal.

6.

Living room. Recording device on table.

GLORIA   Thrilled to be working again. And the role.
              A dream. Which magazine was it?

MAN   The weekend. Colour. Thanks for inviting
              us into your home. Wow.

GLORIA   Do you want?

              CASSIE brings water.

              Water. Thanks Cassie. This is Cassie.

MAN   Hi Cassie.

CASSIE   Hi.

GLORIA   It's on right? You switched it on? *(Meaning
              recording device.)*

MAN	Yes I.
GLORIA	Because.
MAN	It's on.
GLORIA	She's a great help. Aren't you Cassie.

CASSIE laughs faintly.

Because there's nothing worse than half-way through you realise the fucking thing's not even on and all this talking for nothing.

MAN	It's on. See.
GLORIA	Cassie looks after Paul. Our son. You'll meet him.
MAN	Great, I'd like.
GLORIA	And sometimes my husband bends her over and fucks her.

Silence.

MAN	So. The role. How're you finding?
GLORIA	Great to work again. She's just a fuck.
CASSIE	Paul. Let's go play.
GLORIA	A godsend. Don't know what we'd do without. And yes the role. My God. She really.
MAN	Went through hell right? Locked away for how many years? Her own father. I mean that must. Jesus. How do you put yourself in her place? What's that like? Being inside her?

Silence.

GLORIA	Sorry. I.

Pause.

MAN	Do you bring her home?
GLORIA	Sorry?
MAN	You think about her all the time. That cellar. No light. No air. Damp. Disgusting. Jesus. And being back onstage. Nowhere to hide right?
GLORIA	Right. The role's a blessing and Dominic's just great, really supportive. Wants me to dig deep. Expose. Because this story. That poor girl. The father. Like an ape. Ruling his. Living out his. Hell. Absolute.
MAN	Like animals right. Her children. Speaking some kind of made up language?
GLORIA	Their own, yes.
MAN	Horrific. And Dominic. Tell us.
GLORIA	He's one of a kind and we click. Yes there's conflict yes he infuriates me and no it's not always easy or fun but who needs *fun* right. I like to be pushed and I want to go there and he makes things happen which I haven't found with other directors. Can't draw everything out of myself. Need his eye. Even if I make the occasional mistake. *(Laughter.)* He always knows when I need a push or something positive – a compliment – so we can go on.
MAN	Wow.
GLORIA	I only do what I do to please him.
	Pause.
MAN	Right. We just need a few photos. This is Derek.
DEREK	Great place.

GLORIA	Thanks Derek. We're happy here.
DEREK	The view. Really lucky. Shall we.
	They move to the balcony. DEREK *takes photos.*
GLORIA	Close to the sky. With my orange juice in the morning.
	She's unsteady. Supports herself.
	Almost touch it.
DEREK	That's great. Like that.
GLORIA	Like?
	She poses.
DEREK	Good. Let me check. Good. More of that Gloria.
	She poses.
	And to me.
GLORIA	The wind.
DEREK	Like that.
GLORIA	Have we met? Your face.
DEREK	No. I don't think.
GLORIA	Your face is very.
DEREK	But I'm a big fan. Don't move.
	She doesn't move. He shoots.
	That film where you. Italian. The island.
GLORIA	Long time ago.
DEREK	Beautifully shot.
GLORIA	We nearly?

Unsteady.

DEREK   Few inside.

They go in.

Sitting.

The sofa or the bed.

Good. Like that. Sexy. More of that.

GLORIA   I'm all yours, Derek.

Laughter.

DEREK   Keep it like. Good.

GLORIA   You like me, Derek?

Laughter.

Sorry.

Laughter.

DEREK   Is something?

GLORIA   You think I'm hot don't you.

DEREK   Gloria.

GLORIA   Derek.

Only she laughs now.

It's okay. Really.

Still laughing. Too much.

DEREK   Sorry. This.

GLORIA   You want a bit of this?

Her laughter. Suppresses.

Staring at me. With your fucking.

DEREK   Okay. That's.

DEREK	Sorry. I'll be good now, a good girl... Derek.
	Cracks up.
DEREK	This is not what.
GLORIA	What're you staring at fucking pig? You Derek fuck.
	Silence.
MAN	Get a couple with the son.
CASSIE	Wait.
	She brings PAUL. Straightens his hair.
MAN	Next to her.
CASSIE	Here Paul. Next to mummy.
	PAUL sits next to GLORIA. DEREK shoots.
DEREK	Good.
MAN	Both real serious.
DEREK	That's good.
	Checks the display on his camera.
	Nice and formal. Mother and son. Good.
MAN	Is she alright?
CASSIE	She's fine. Tired.
MAN	Okay. Couple more.

7.

Living room.

CASSIE	They're cancelling – *postponing* – the premiere. She's a mess. They never know if she'll turn up, what state. Drunk,

destructive. I'm worried about Paul. It's not
right. His mother. She wants you back. She
doesn't care what happened.

JARED   Cassie.

CASSIE   She actually thinks it'll still go ahead. She
             wants to wear the dress you gave her. She
             wants you there. On her arm afterwards.
             I'm sorry. Everything.

JARED   You looked so hot. In the mirror, in her new
             dress. It was nice but it meant nothing.

             Pause.

             I'll be back later to pick Paul up.

CASSIE   Heard you got promoted.

JARED   My own unit.

CASSIE   Congratulations.

JARED   Thank you.

8.

Living room.

GLORIA alone. The television. PAUL enters. In his pyjamas. Sleepy.

PAUL   Can't sleep.

             He cuddles up to her on the couch.

GLORIA   It's okay darling. Just lie here with Mummy.

PAUL   Who are they fighting?

GLORIA   Bad guys.

PAUL   I had nightmares.

GLORIA   It's okay, sweetheart.

PAUL	Fog. I couldn't see. I got lost, couldn't find our door.
GLORIA	You're safe now.
	She cradles him.

9.

Living room.

GLORIA	I saw you on TV. You both looked happy. Smiling for the cameras. Your new life. Congratulations. All those medals. Cassie was watching too. You know I think she felt something for you. That you actually *cared* for her. Poor girl.
JARED	Gloria.
GLORIA	You've done well. A general's daughter.
JARED	I want Paul to live with me and Jacinta. This is not a good environment for him.
GLORIA	Sometimes on television, there's a blast. Windows blown out. A building like ours. But it's not. Will the fighting be over soon?
JARED	Where is he?
GLORIA	With Cassie. In the park. We can.
	Pause.
	If you want.
	He runs his fingers through her hair.
	I won't tell.
	They kiss.
	You can do anything you want.
JARED	Gloria.

GLORIA	A what-do-you-call-it? Mercy fuck.
JARED	I.
GLORIA	Like when we first met. Except it hurts.
JARED	I want my son to come and live with me. I don't want him near you.
	Silence.
	We're finished. Do you understand?
	She nods.

10.

Living room.

PAUL is playing his video game. MADDIE watches.

PAUL	Want a go?
MADDIE	No thanks.
	GLORIA enters carrying a present. She kisses PAUL on the head. He keeps playing his game. GLORIA stares at MADDIE.
GLORIA	I don't know you.
MADDIE	I'm Maddie. Remember.
GLORIA	Maddie?
MADDIE	My mum, she.
GLORIA	*(Screaming.)* Cassie!
	CASSIE runs in.
	Who's she?
CASSIE	You remember Maddie. My daughter Maddie.
	Pause.

	No-one to look after her today so she's hanging out with me, right Maddie?
MADDIE	What's that? *(Meaning the present.)*
CASSIE	Sweetheart come help Mum stack the dishwasher. We're going soon.
GLORIA	Oh this. For Paul.
CASSIE	Look darling, Mummy got you a present.

CASSIE switches off the game.

PAUL	What is it?
CASSIE	Open and see.

He just holds it in his hands and stares at it.

MADDIE	Open it.

PAUL opens the present – the tin bird.

GLORIA	You can make it fly.

PAUL does nothing, just stares at the bird.

You squeeze the handle. The wings. To make it fly.

He does.

(To CASSIE.) His father is collecting him tomorrow. There's no more work for you here.

12.

Living room.

Night. GLORIA watching TV. Sound on mute. PAUL enters and sits beside her. Nothing for a long time, then she walks to the kitchen, opens the fridge, stares inside. Finally, she pours a glass of milk which he drinks, still watching the television. When he's finished, she rinses the glass and puts it in the dishwasher. She takes a long, sharp kitchen knife from the drawer and sits back down. PAUL snuggles into her. She strokes his hair. They watch television. She cradles him, kisses his head. Stares at the television.

GLORIA   He's out there. In the dust and green light. In rooms where terrified people cover their heads. Like this –

She demonstrates.

Dead eyes. Sex. Perfume.

Pause.

Once he held her and whispered *my queen.* The boy their everything. His breath is hot against her neck. Little chest rising, falling. The kitchen knife is a splinter of ice in her hand. Her thoughts crowd around it. She's doing this. Because she loves him. Calm now. A slice. Listen. Air sucked from room. Little body heavier. Lays him down. Kisses his eyes. Full of love.

She lays him down and closes his eyes.

13.

Living room.

PAUL's body is put in a body bag by police officers. A forensic officer takes photos of the scene.

14.

Empty stage.

GLORIA   I stand upstage of the curtain. Listening to the audience. That hum. Does it even have a name? The house lights dim. Silence.

Fade.

Five.

1.

Family Room.

MADDIE is nursing a newborn baby.

DEREK	Ready sweetheart?
	Laughter.
MADDIE	You start.
	Laughter.
DEREK	No you.
	Laughter.
MADDIE	*(Quietly.)* Oh look. We woke her up. Hello. Hello little one.
	Pause.
	No. Actually, we don't go down there much.
DEREK	Not anymore. No.
MADDIE	Not safe.
DEREK	Nah not really safe.
	Pause.
	Totally happy here. Yep. Everything we need. Each other.
	Laughter.
MADDIE	Got it all. Her.
DEREK	Each other. The view.

MADDIE	Out there with my orange juice. Close to the sky. Who'd want to live down there?
DEREK	People look up and want what we've got. The view. Clean. Safe.
MADDIE	We're lucky.
DEREK	It's different from where other people live. More comfortable. And higher up.
	Laughter.
MADDIE	*(To the baby.)* Hello. Mummy's little girl. Say hello.
DEREK	Where's Paul? Paul. Paul.
MADDIE	Yes. Terrible. Her own. I can't bear to.
DEREK	We don't.
MADDIE	How any mother.
DEREK	Didn't hear a thing, no. *(Calling.)* Paul. Dinner.

2.

PAUL's room.

PAUL	I walk room to room. No-one shoots back. No-one's screaming. It's calm. I place the shots wherever I like. Head or body. Leg if I want them to fall first. So I don't get bored. So each kill doesn't feel the same.

3.

Studio.

CASSIE	*(Smiling.)* Like this?
AD	They want more smile.

CASSIE	*(Smiles more.)*
AD	Think about the people at home.
CASSIE	Huh?
AD	On their sofas. Eating dinner. Teeth. Smile.
	CASSIE stares and smiles.
	Happy happy. Warm inside. Twirling the ribbons. Good. And – we're done.
CASSIE	How was it?
AD	Great. Hold on, they need one more. Okay, you're putting the packet in the trolley. You've made your decision. You're happy. You love life. You made the right decision and your family will love you for it. Good Cassie. Okay down the barrel and smile.
	CASSIE smiles.
	Good. That's it. Good girl.

4.

Ship cabin.

JARED	I look back to shore. The harbour. Black mirror. Lights. Everyone wants to live up there now. Close to sky. I've forgotten them. Don't even dream them. Then I'm walking the streets of some city, in the crowd or shop window, her face, a split-second ghostly gone again, or I'm fucking a woman I paid to love me in some port and suddenly her face is right there.
	Silence.
	On the TV fixed to the wall of my cabin, a woman is crying. News or documentary.

272

She's in jail. One of those tables you know
with the glass. Sound mute. I can't stop
staring. Her face is a cavern. I need to sleep.
Tonight I'll sleep. Jesus. Her face.

5.

Cell.

GLORIA   You want me to describe how it felt. At you
or the camera? Not my best. At you. Like
a conversation. Okay. Like this? Music.
Listen. What? Sorry. Yes of course I'm
ready.

Her face.

Slow fade.

The author would like to thank
Marius von Mayenburg, Matthew Whittet,
Ralph Myers, Alice Babidge, Maja Zade,
Howard Gooding, Jean Mostyn, Mark Subias,
Brian and Judy Andrews, Mary-Elizabeth Andrews,
and Margrét Bjarnadóttir.

Benedict Andrews is a multi-award winning director of theatre and opera. He is known for iconoclastic stagings of masterpieces by Shakespeare, Chekhov, Tennessee Williams and Jean Genet, as well as plays by cutting edge contemporary writers. As a writer, his adaptations include versions of *The Seagull*, *Three Sisters*, *The Maids*, *Life is a Dream* (with Beatrix Christian), and *War of the Roses* (with Tom Wright). Benedict's first feature film, *Una*, will be released in 2016. His book of poetry, *Lens Flare* (Pitt Street Poetry) received the 2016 Mary Gilmore Prize.

www.benedictandrews.com

www.ingramcontent.com/pod-product-compliance
Ingram Content Group UK Ltd.
Pitfield, Milton Keynes, MK11 3LW, UK
UKHW031249020325
455689UK00008B/136